Wiley CPAexcel® Exam Review

PRACTICE QUESTIONS

2019

BUSINESS ENVIRONMENT AND CONCEPTS

Wiley CPAexcel® Exam Review

PRACTICE QUESTIONS

2019

BUSINESS ENVIRONMENT AND CONCEPTS

Allen Bizzell, Ph.D., CPA (inactive)
Robert A. Prentice, J.D.
Dan N. Stone, Ph.D. CPA (inactive)

Wiley Efficient Learning™

ISBN 978-1-119-53446-4
ISBN 978-1-119-53447-1 (ebk); ISBN 978-1-119-53448-8 (ebk)

Printed in the United States of America.

V10004723_092818

Table of Contents

Multiple Choice Questions

Corporate Governance

Internal Control Frameworks

Introduction to COSO, Internal Control, and the COSO Cube

aicpa.aq.intro.coso.int.ctrl.003_17

1. Which of the following statements is **true** regarding internal control objectives of information systems?

   A. Primary responsibility of viable internal control rests with the internal audit division.
   B. A secure system may have inherent risks due to management's analysis of trade-offs identified by cost-benefit studies.
   C. Control objectives primarily emphasize output distribution issues.
   D. An entity's corporate culture is irrelevant to the objectives.

aq.intro.coso.int.ctrl.001

2. Gimbly Cricket Corp. created a decision aid, linked to its data warehouse, to enable senior management to monitor, in real time, changes in oil production at its oil wells in Kazakhstan. This is an example of:

   A. Internal, financial reporting
   B. Internal, nonfinancial reporting.
   C. External, financial reporting.
   D. External, nonfinancial reporting.

aicpa.aq.intro.coso.int.ctrl.004_2-18

3. According to COSO, which of the following components addresses the need to respond in an organized manner to significant changes resulting from international exposure, acquisitions, or executive transitions?

   A. Control activities
   B. Risk assessment
   C. Monitoring activities
   D. Information and communication

AICPA.101043BEC-SIM

4. In the COSO (2011) "cube" model, each of the following are components of internal control except

   A. Monitoring.
   B. Control activities.
   C. Operations control.
   D. Risk assessment.

AICPA.130522BEC-SIM

5. This fundamental component of internal control is the core or foundation of any system of internal control.

   A. Control activities.
   B. Control environment.
   C. Information and communication.
   D. Risk assessment.

AICPA.130526BEC-SIM

6. This is the process of identifying, analyzing, and managing the risks involved in achieving the organization's objectives.

   A. Control activities.
   B. Control environment.
   C. Information and communication.
   D. Risk assessment.

AICPA.130719BEC

7. According to COSO, which of the following is a compliance objective?

   A. To maintain adequate staffing to keep overtime expense within budget.
   B. To maintain a safe level of carbon dioxide emissions during production.
   C. To maintain material price variances within published guidelines.
   D. To maintain accounting principles that conform to GAAP.

17 Principles of Internal Control

aicpa.aq.coso.17prcpls.003_17

8. Employees of an entity feel peer pressure to do the right thing; management appropriately deals with signs that problems exist and resolves the issues; and dealings with customers, suppliers, employees, and other parties are based on honesty and fairness. According to COSO, the above scenario is indicative of which of the following?

   A. Strategic goals
   B. Operational excellence
   C. Reporting reliability
   D. Tone at the top

aq.coso.17prcpls.001

9. Management of Johnson Company is considering implementing technology to improve the monitoring of internal control. Which of the following **best** describes how technology may be effective at improving internal control monitoring?

    A. Technology can identify conditions and circumstances that indicate that controls have failed or risks are present.
    B. Technology can ensure that items are processed accurately.
    C. Technology can provide information more quickly.
    D. Technology can control access to terminals and data.

aq.coso.17prcpls.002

10. Henry Higgins of Jiffy Grill has learned that the controller is likely embezzling money to fund an expensive drug and gambling habit. Ideally, Henry should communicate this information to:

    A. The controller.
    B. His boss.
    C. An anonymous hotline set up by Jiffy Grill.
    D. His employees.

AICPA.130517BEC-SIM

11. According to the 17 COSO control principles, information quality primarily relates to which fundamental component of internal control:

    A. Control activities.
    B. Control environment.
    C. Information and communication.
    D. Monitoring.

Types and Limitations of Accounting Controls

aq.types.limit.acct.cont.001

12. Which of the following is a general control rather than a transaction control activity?

    A. Technology development policies and procedures.
    B. Reconciliations.
    C. Physical controls over assets.
    D. Controls over standing data.

aq.types.limit.acct.cont.002

13. Which of the following is **not** a limitation of internal control?

    A. Human judgment in decision making may be faulty.
    B. External forces may attack the system.
    C. Management may override internal control.
    D. Controls may be circumvented by collusion.

AICPA.040213BEC-SIM

14. Which of the following is an example of a detective control?

    A. Use of pre-formatted screens for data entry.
    B. Comparison of data entry totals to batch control totals.
    C. Restricting access to the computer operations center to data-processing staff only.
    D. Employing a file librarian to maintain custody of the program and data files.

AICPA.090774.BEC

15. Controls in the information technology area are classified into the categories of preventive, detective, and corrective. Which of the following is a preventive control?

    A. Contingency planning.
    B. Hash total.
    C. Echo check.
    D. Access control software.

AICPA.120613BEC

16. Which of the following statements presents an example of a general control for a computerized system?

    A. Limiting entry of sales transactions to only valid credit customers.
    B. Creating hash totals from Social Security numbers for the weekly payroll.
    C. Restricting entry of accounts payable transactions to only authorized users.
    D. Restricting access to the computer center by use of biometric devices.

AICPA.130716BEC

17. A company's new time clock process requires hourly employees to select an identification number and then choose the clock-in or clock-out button. A video camera captures an image of the employee using the system. Which of the following exposures can the new system be expected to change the **least**?

    A. Fraudulent reporting of employees' own hours.
    B. Errors in employees' overtime computation.
    C. Inaccurate accounting of employees' hours.
    D. Recording of other employees' hours.

Internal Control Roles and Responsibilities

aicpa.aq.inter.cont.roles.respon.004_17

18. According to COSO, the presence of a written code of conduct provides for a control environment that can

    A. Override an entity's history and culture.
    B. Encourage teamwork in the pursuit of an entity's objectives.
    C. Ensure that competent evaluators are implementing and monitoring internal controls.
    D. Verify that information systems are providing persuasive evidence of the effectiveness of internal controls.

aq.inter.cont.roles.respon.001

19. According to the COSO internal control framework, if an organization outsources certain activities within the business to an outside party:

    A. Responsibility also transfers to the outside party.
    B. The responsibilities never transfer to the outsourced party.
    C. The responsibilities only transfer if the outside party explicitly agrees to accept responsibility.
    D. The organization is no longer accountable for the outsourced activities.

aq.inter.cont.roles.respon.002

20. The IT department at Piggy Parts BBQ has recently learned of phishing attempts that rely on social engineering to break into its financial systems. Information about these attempts should be communicated to:

    A. Internal auditors.
    B. Other personnel.
    C. All personnel.
    D. Support functions.

aq.inter.cont.roles.respon.003

21. Jiffy Grill has an ERP system. It has assigned responsibility for determining who has what access rights within the ERP system. This assignment mostly likely was to:

    A. Internal auditors.
    B. Other personnel.
    C. Management
    D. Support functions

Internal Control Monitoring—Purpose and Terminology

aicpa.aq.coso.erm2.003_17

22. According to COSO, a primary purpose of monitoring internal control is to verify that the internal control system remains adequate to address changes in

    A. Risks.
    B. The law.
    C. Technology.
    D. Operating procedures.

aicpa.aq.coso.erm2.004_17

23. The materials manager of a warehouse is given a new product line to manage with new inventory control procedures. Which of the following sequences of the COSO internal control monitoring-for-change continuum is affected by the new product line?

    A. Control baseline but not change management
    B. Change management but not control baseline
    C. Neither control baseline nor change management
    D. Both control baseline and change management

aq.coso.erm2.001

24. According to the COSO framework, evaluators who monitor controls within an organization should have which of the following sets of characteristics?

    A. Competence and objectivity.
    B. Respect and judgment.
    C. Judgment and objectivity.
    D. Authority and responsibility.

aq.coso.erm2.002

25. Jeffrey Smiggles of Rajon Rondo Sportswear has developed a software application that helps monitor key production risks at company factories. In order to reduce costs, his approach to monitoring risks is likely to be:

    A. Monitor all risks using indirect information.
    B. Monitor all risks using direct information.
    C. Monitor more important risks using indirect information and less important risks using direct information.
    D. Monitor more important risks using direct information and less important risks using indirect information

AICPA.110533BEC-SIM

26. Which of the following are reasons that internal controls need to be monitored?

    A. People forget, quit jobs, get lazy, or come to work hung over.
    B. Machines fail.
    C. Advances in technology.
    D. All of the above.

AICPA.110534BEC-SIM

27. Which of the following is the best definition of a compensating control?

    A. A control that accomplishes the same objective as another control.
    B. A condition within an internal control system requiring attention.
    C. The targets against which the effectiveness of internal control are evaluated.
    D. Metrics that reflect critical success factors.

AICPA.130723BEC

28. Within the COSO Internal Control—Integrated Framework, which of the following components is designed to ensure that internal controls continue to operate effectively?

    A. Control environment.
    B. Risk assessment.
    C. Information and communication.
    D. Monitoring.

Internal Control Monitoring and Change Control Processes

aq.inte.cont.monit.proces.001

29. A change control process would likely **not** include which of the following?

    A. Change request form.
    B. Approval process.
    C. Outsourcing.
    D. Documentation.

aq.inte.cont.monit.proces.003

30. Ashley's Tree and Trim has an automated system that monitors system access events and reports them, in real time, to the IT security manager. This type of monitoring is:

    A. Continuous.
    B. Self.
    C. XBRL-enabled.
    D. Supervisory.

AICPA.120621BEC

31. In a large public corporation, evaluating internal control procedures should be the responsibility of

    A. Accounting management staff who report to the CFO.
    B. Internal audit staff who report to the board of directors.
    C. Operations management staff who report to the chief operations officer.
    D. Security management staff who report to the chief facilities officer.

Enterprise Risk Management Frameworks

Introduction to COSO Enterprise Risk Management: Strategy and Risk

aq.erm.intro.strat.001_2-18

32. Match the statements below with the associated categories in ERM:

    1. We will improve the quality of life of …
    2. We will be known for outstanding …
    3. We will treat our customers and employees with respect …

    A. 1 core values, 2 risk appetite, 3 mission
    B. 1 strategy, 2 values, 3 vision
    C. 1 tolerance, 2 mission, 3 appetite
    D. 1 mission, 2 vision, 3 core values

aq.erm.intro.strat.002_2-18

33. Demanding higher performance usually requires accepting more _____.

    A. Tolerance
    B. Vision
    C. Risk
    D. Performance severity

aq.erm.intro.strat.004_2-18

34. The ERM component that includes email, board meeting minutes, and reports as important elements is

    A. Governance and Culture.
    B. Performance.
    C. Review and Revision.
    D. Information, Communication, and Reporting.

ERM Components, Principles, and Terms

aq.erm.comp.princ.001_2-18

35. AppleNCheese Food Products recently completed a systematic analysis of the political, economic, social, technological, legal, and environmental conditions that it expects in the short and the long term. This analysis most likely occurs as a part of which component in the ERM framework?

   A. Governance and Culture
   B. Performance
   C. Strategy and Objective-Setting
   D. Information, Communication, and Reporting

aq.erm.comp.princ.002_2-18

36. BigWig Costume Rentals recently implemented an initiative to attract and retain web programmers and systems analysts as a part of its expanded web development to support online sales. This initiative most likely occurs as a part of which component in the ERM framework?

   A. Governance and Culture
   B. Performance
   C. Strategy and Objective-Setting
   D. Information, Communication, and Reporting

aq.erm.comp.princ.003_2-18

37. Dennis Rodman's Shoes and Shinola recently implemented a whistleblower hotline to facilitate the reporting of events and concerns related to potential violations of its code of conduct. This initiative most likely occurs as a part of which component in the ERM framework?

   A. Governance and Culture
   B. Performance
   C. Strategy and Objective-Setting
   D. Information, Communication, and Reporting

ERM Governance and Culture

aq.erm.gov.cult.001_2-18

38. According to the COSO ERM framework, which of the following is least likely to impede the independence of a board member?

   A. Jane was a partner at the accounting firm that conducted the organization's financial statement audit five years ago but has no existing business or contractual relationships with the entity or its key stakeholders currently.

   B. June has a material consulting contract with the organization related to facilitating marketing and sales promotion.
   C. Laura is a board member of the organization's major competitor.
   D. Megan has served on the board for 15 years.

aq.erm.gov.cult.002_2-18

39. Frequently in an organization with a dual board of directors structure,

   A. The management committee oversees strategy while the governing board oversees operations.
   B. The management board oversees operations while the governing board oversees strategy.
   C. The under-board oversees operations while the over-board oversees strategy.
   D. The management board manages the risk portfolio while the chief risk officer coordinates risk.

aq.erm.gov.cult.003_2-18

40. In a risk-aware organization,

   A. The organizational culture is independent of management.
   B. The organizational culture will be risk averse.
   C. Investments in unproven technologies will be minimized.
   D. The organizational culture is closely linked to the organization's strategy, objectives, and business context.

aq.erm.gov.cult.004_2-18

41. Which of the following is an important threat to accountability in an organization's ERM practices?

   A. Excessive communication
   B. Hypocrisy (i.e., when management says one thing and does another)
   C. Escalation
   D. Deviations

ERM Strategy and Objective Setting

aq.erm.obj.set.001_2-18

42. In ERM, _____ focuses on the development of strategy and goals while _____ focuses on the implementation of strategy and variation from plans.

   A. tolerance; triggers
   B. key indicators; risk appetite
   C. risk appetite; tolerance
   D. internal control; portfolio view of risk

aq.erm.obj.set.002_2-18

43. Which of the following statements of risk appetite related to factory floor accidents is acceptable?

    "Low"
    " < 3 per year"

    A. Neither
    B. Both
    C. "Low" but not " <3 per year."
    D. "< 3 per year" but not "Low."

aq.erm.obj.set.003_2-18

44. An investment firm determines that investments in bitcoin are highly risky. For its portfolio, it sets a minimum investment of 3% and a maximum investment of 8% in bitcoin. This is an example of setting

    A. risk target (minimum) and risk roof (maximum).
    B. risk roof (minimum) and risk target (maximum).
    C. risk floor (minimum) and risk ceiling (maximum).
    D. risk ceiling (minimum) and risk floor (maximum).

ERM and Performance

aq.erm.performance.001_2-18

45. A heat map used as a part of assessing risks plots the_____ on the vertical axis against the_____ on the horizontal axis.

    A. likelihood rating; impact ratings
    B. inherent risk; risk appetite
    C. target residual risk, actual residual risk
    D. internal control; inherent risk

aq.erm.performance.002_2-18

46. Match each statement below with the appropriate term that best describes it:

    I. After considering implemented controls, the desired level of the risk of a major cyber attack is low.
    II. Before considering controls, the level of risk of a major cyber attack is high.
    III. After considering implemented controls, the level of the risk of a major cyber attack is medium.

    A. Internal control; inherent risk; target residual risk
    B. target residual risk; internal control; inherent risk

    C. target residual risk; actual residual risk; assessed risk
    D. target residual risk; inherent risk; actual residual risk

CGIC-0047B

47. Management of Warren Company has decided to respond to a particular risk by hedging the risk with futures contracts. This is an example of risk

    A. Avoidance.
    B. Acceptance.
    C. Reduction.
    D. Sharing.

ERM Monitoring, Review, and Revision

aq.erm.monitor.rev.001_2-18

48. Which of the following is least likely to trigger a review and revision to an organization's ERM practices?

    A. The purchase and implementation of a system that enables real-time monitoring of customer satisfaction and complaints.
    B. A sales growth rate that is 2½ times that which was expected.
    C. A 4% increase in calls to the whistleblower hotline.
    D. Firing the CRO.

aq.erm.monitor.rev.002_2-18

49. An organization launches a new product and finds the product is performing better than expected and that the volatility of sales is less than expected. Which of the following is the organization most likely to do?

    A. Review its internal control procedures.
    B. Investigate new technologies to improve product performance.
    C. Revise its tolerance and decrease its risk appetite
    D. Review its ERM practices.

aq.erm.monitor.rev.003_2-18

50. An entity reviews its ERM practices. Which question is the organization least likely to investigate as a part of this review?

    A. What is the relationship between our strategy and objectives?
    B. How did the entity perform?
    C. Are we taking sufficient risks to attain desired performance?
    D. Were risk estimates accurate?

ERM Communication and Reporting

aq.erm.comm.report.001_2-18

51. Data from _____ is typically structured, while data from _____ is typically unstructured.

   A. board meeting minutes; a governmental water scarcity report that is used by a beverage company
   B. staffing increases or decreases due to restructuring; email about decision making and performance.
   C. emerging interest in a new product from a competitor; an entity's risk tolerance
   D. marketing reports from website tracking services; government-produced geopolitical reports and studies

aq.erm.comm.report.002_2-18

52. Key risk indicators are

   A. Indicators of internal control quality.
   B. Substantively equivalent to KPIs.
   C. Predictive and usually quantitative.
   D. Used primarily by risk-aware, risk-averse entities.

aq.erm.comm.report.003_2-18

53. Riley, Ripley, and RudBack are builders of high-end (i.e., expensive) customized homes. They want to create a report on the risks that they face in their human resources function. Which level of reporting would be appropriate to this goal?

   A. Portfolio view
   B. Risk view
   C. Risk category view
   D. Risk profile view

Fraud Risk Management

aicpa.aq.ent.fraud.mgmt.008_2-18

54. In a small public company that has few levels of management with wide spans of control, each of the following mitigates management override of controls **except**

   A. Establishing an effective and anonymous whistleblower program with which employees can feel comfortable reporting any irregularities.
   B. Establishing a corporate culture in which integrity and ethical values are highly appreciated.
   C. Having two officers who significantly influence management and operations.
   D. Having an effective internal auditor function.

aq.ent.fraud.mgmt.002_17

55. Griswold Corp. is planning a data analytics program to manage the risk of vendor fraud in purchasing. Which of the following activities would occur last in this process?

   A. Determine the risk of management override of controls over purchases.
   B. Determine reporting procedures for vendor anomalies.
   C. Screen data to remove html tags from harvested vendor data.
   D. Validate scraped data to match to existing vendor files.

aq.ent.fraud.mgmt.003_17

56. The Greensburg Agriculture Products employee survey related to fraud includes this statement: "We are discouraged from sharing our computer passwords with others." This statement best relates to which of the following fraud management principles and processes?

   A. Establishing a fraud risk management program
   B. Selecting, developing, and deploying fraud controls
   C. Selecting, developing, and deploying evaluation and monitoring processes
   D. Establishing a communication program to obtain information about potential frauds

aq.ent.fraud.mgmt.004_17

57. Overland Stage and Transport uses a fraud risk assessment heat map that charts the significance (on the vertical axis) and the likelihood (on the horizontal axis) of frauds as a part of its fraud risk management program. The company's use of a fraud risk heat map best relates to which of the following activities?

   A. Establishing a fraud risk management program
   B. Selecting, developing, and deploying fraud controls
   C. Selecting, developing, and deploying evaluation and monitoring processes
   D. Performing a comprehensive fraud risk assessment

Other Regulatory Frameworks and Provisions

aicpa.aq.oth.reg.fram.gov.008_17

58. Which of the following statements is correct regarding the requirements of the Sarbanes-Oxley Act of 2002 for an issuer's board of directors?

   A. Each member of the board of directors must be independent from management influence, based on the member's prior and current activities, economic and family relationships, and other factors.
   B. The board of directors must have an audit committee entirely composed of members who are independent from management influence.
   C. The majority of members of the board of directors must be independent from management influence.
   D. The board of directors must have a compensation committee, a nominating committee, and an audit committee, each of which is composed entirely of independent members.

aq.oth.reg.fram.gov.001_2017

59. In a public company, which of the following officers must certify that the accuracy of their firms' financial statements as filed with the SEC?

   A. CEO and CAO
   B. CAO and CFO
   C. CFO and CEO
   D. CEO and COO

aq.oth.reg.fram.gov.002_2017

60. Public company CEOs and CFOs must certify that:

   A. They are responsible for establishing and maintaining their firm's internal financial controls.
   B. They have hired an excellent auditing firm and have delegated to that firm ultimate responsibility for the accuracy of financial statements.
   C. They have taken lie detector tests regarding the accuracy of the financial statements.
   D. They are subject to firm codes of ethics policing the accuracy of financial statements.

aq.oth.reg.fram.gov.003_2017

61. Public company external audit firms must audit their clients':

   A. Financial statements.
   B. Internal controls.
   C. Financial statements and internal controls.
   D. Neither financial statements nor internal controls.

aq.oth.reg.fram.gov.004_2017

62. Every audit committee of a public company must have at least one:

   A. Legal expert who understands the liabilities that public companies can face if they misreport financial information.
   B. Financial expert who understands GAAP and financial statements.
   C. Ethics expert who is familiar with Immanuel Kant's writings.
   D. Accounting expert who is familiar with the AICPA Code of Professional Conduct.

aq.oth.reg.fram.gov.005_2017

63. CFO Mar has been complicit in her public company's accounting fraud. She consults a lawyer as it becomes time for filing her firm's 10-K with the SEC. She is a little uncomfortable about what she might have to do. The lawyer will likely tell her that she will have to certify (and be potentially criminally liable for lying about) all of the following matters except:

   A. That she has reviewed the 10-K.
   B. That her CPA license is active.
   C. That she, along with the CEO, is responsible for establishing and maintaining her company's internal controls.
   D. That she has recently evaluated the effectiveness of the firm's internal controls.

aq.oth.reg.fram.gov.006_2017

64. Public company audit committees must contain which of the following?

   A. A majority of independent directors
   B. An accounting expert
   C. A financial expert
   D. A legal expert

aq.oth.reg.fram.gov.007_2017

65. A public company audit committee's "financial expert" must have all of the following except:

   A. An understanding of GAAP and financial statements.
   B. Experience in preparing or auditing financial statements of comparable companies and application of such principles in connection with accounting for estimates, accruals, and reserves.
   C. Experience with internal auditing controls.
   D. Experience on a public company's compensation committee.

aq.oth.reg.fram.gov.009_17

66. Which of the following organizations was established by the Sarbanes-Oxley Act of 2002 to control the auditing profession?

    A. Information Systems Audit and Control Foundation (ISACF)
    B. IT Governance Institute (ITGI)
    C. Public Company Accounting Oversight Board (PCAOB)
    D. Committee of Sponsoring Organizations (COSO)

aq.oth.reg.fram.gov.010_17

67. Which of the following situations most clearly illustrates a breach of fiduciary duty by one or more members of the board of directors of a corporation?

    A. A corporation previously has distributed 50% of its earnings as dividends. This year it has annual earnings per share of $2, and the board of directors voted 4 to 1 against paying any dividend to finance growth.
    B. A director of a corporation who co-owns a computer vendor negotiated the purchase of a computer system by the corporation from the vendor, making a disclosure to the corporation and the other board members. The purchase price was competitive, and the board (absent the vendor co-owner) unanimously approved the purchase.
    C. Two directors of a corporation favor business expansion, two oppose it, and the fifth did not attend the meeting. During the five years that the fifth person has been a director, the individual did **not** attend two other meetings.
    D. A director who learned that the corporation is thinking of buying retail space in a city personally purchased a vacant building in the same city that would have been suitable for use by the corporation.

Economic Concepts and Analysis

Introduction to Economic Concepts

AICPA.082253BEC.EM.I.I

68. The following graph shows four curves: A-A, B-B, C-C, and D-D.

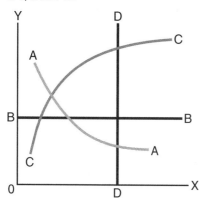

Which of these curves depict variables that are not interdependent?

	A-A	B-B	C-C	D-D
A.	Yes	Yes	Yes	Yes
B.	Yes	No	Yes	No
C.	No	Yes	No	Yes
D.	Yes	Yes	Yes	No

AICPA.090478BEC-SIM

69. Which of the following statements regarding the use of graphs to depict economic relationships is not correct?

A. When the dependent variable moves in the same manner or direction as the independent variable, then the relationship between the variables is positive.
B. When the dependent variable does not change as the independent variable changes, the relationship between the variables is neutral.
C. The plotted relationship between variables shown in graph form can be negative, as well as positive.
D. The vertical axis of an economic graph is referred to as the X axis.

AICPA.090481BEC-SIM

70. Measures of the economic activity of an entire nation would be included in the study of

A. Microeconomics.
B. Macroeconomics.
C. International economics.
D. Governmental economics.

Microeconomics

Introduction and Free-Market Model

AICPA.090482BEC-SIM

71. In a free-market economy, which of the following should be the least significant factor in determining resource allocation and use?

A. Preferences of individuals.
B. Availability of economic resources.
C. Government regulation of commerce.
D. Level of technological development.

AICPA.090483BEC-SIM

72. The free-market economy flow model depicts four major interrelated flows:

I. Individuals provide economic resources to business firms.
II. Firms provide payment to individuals for economic resources.
III. Firms provide goods and services to individuals.
IV. Individuals provide payment to firms for goods and services.

If financial institutions and businesses suddenly and severely restrict the availability of consumer credit, which one of the above flows would be most likely to be the first to be impacted adversely?

A. I.
B. II.
C. III.
D. IV.

AICPA0811629BEC.III.E

73. Which of the following are considered economic resources?

	Labor	Capital	Natural Resources
A.	Yes	Yes	Yes
B.	Yes	Yes	No
C.	Yes	No	No
D.	No	Yes	Yes

Demand

AICPA.090486BEC-SIM

74. Concurrent with a significant downturn in the economy, the sale of Scope's high-end electronics decreased dramatically. Which of the following is the most likely direct cause of the decline in demand for Scope's products?

   A. Scope increased the price of the products.
   B. Income of market participants decreased.
   C. Scope reduced the price of its products.
   D. Market participants' preferences for electronics changes.

AICPA.130712BEC

75. The demand curve for a product reflects which of the following?

   A. The impact of prices on the amount of product offered.
   B. The willingness of producers to offer a product at alternative prices.
   C. The impact that price has on the amount of a product purchased.
   D. The impact that price has on the purchase amount of two related products.

assess.AICPA.BEC.micro.demand-0020

76. Increased demand for product A increases the demand for resources used to produce product A. What is the best explanation for the increase in the demand for resources?

   A. The theory of derived demand is working.
   B. Product A is in an expanding industry.
   C. The theory of the invisible hand is working.
   D. The demand for product A is highly elastic.

Supply

AICPA.090487BEC-SIM

77. In the statement "quantity supplied is a function of price," are the variables quantity and price dependent or independent variables?

	Quantity	Price
A.	Independent	Independent
B.	Independent	Dependent
C.	Dependent	Independent
D.	Dependent	Dependent

AICPA.090488BEC-SIM

78. If a change in market variables causes a supply curve to shift inward, which one of the following will occur?

   A. The price at which the same quantity will be provided after the shift will be less than the price before the shift.
   B. At a given price, a greater quantity will be provided after the shift than the quantity provided before the shift.
   C. The supply curve after the shift will intercept the Y axis at a lower point than before the shift.
   D. In order for the same quantity to be provided after the shift as was provided before the shift, price will have to increase.

AICPA.090489BEC-SIM

79. When the cost of input factors to the production process increases, which one of the following will occur?

   A. The demand curve will shift outward.
   B. The supply curve will shift outward.
   C. The demand curve will shift inward.
   D. The supply curve will shift inward.

Market Equilibrium

aq.micro.equil.001

80. An increase in the market supply of beef would result in a/an

   A. increase in the price of beef.
   B. decrease in the demand for beef.
   C. increase in the price of pork.
   D. increase in the quantity of beef demanded.

AICPA.130738BEC-SIM

81. A price ceiling that is below the market equilibrium price would be expected to result in which one of the following sets of effects on demand and supply?

	Supply	Demand
A.	Excess	Shortage
B.	Excess	Excess
C.	Shortage	Shortage
D.	Shortage	Excess

Elasticity

aq.micro.elas.001_2017

82. Tower Inc. sells a product that is a close substitute for a product offered by Westco. Historically, management of Tower has observed a coefficient of cross-elasticity of 1.5 between the two products. If management of Tower anticipates a 5% increase in price by Westco, how would this action by Westco's management be expected to affect the demand for Tower's product?

   A. A 5% increase.
   B. A 5% decrease.
   C. A 7.5% increase.
   D. A 7.5% decrease.

aq.micro.elas.002_2017

83. Which of the following characteristics would indicate that an item sold would have a high price elasticity of demand?

   A. The item has many similar substitutes.
   B. The cost of the item is low compared to the total budget of the purchasers.
   C. The item is considered a necessity.
   D. Changes in the price of the item are regulated by governmental agency.

AICPA.090493BEC-SIM

84. A 4% increase in the market price of Commodity X resulted in an 8% increase in the quantity of Commodity X supplied. Which one of the following statements is correct?

   A. Supply is inelastic.
   B. Supply is unitary.
   C. Supply is elastic.
   D. Supply is price neutral.

Consumer Demand and Utility Theory

aq.micro.cnsmr.dmnd.001_2017

85. When maximizing utility in economics, what is being maximized?

   A. Profits.
   B. Satisfaction.
   C. Costs.
   D. Elasticity.

AICPA.090496BEC-SIM

86. Allen buys only beer and pizza. When the price of beer is $2.00 per bottle and the price of pizza is $10.00, Allen maximizes his total utility (satisfaction) by buying 5 beers and 4 pizzas. If the marginal utility of the 5th beer is 100 utils, which one of the following would be the marginal utility of the 4th pizza?

   A. 40 utils.
   B. 100 utils.
   C. 200 utils.
   D. 500 utils.

AICPA.130739BEC-SIM

87. Allen has the following schedule of marginal utility for slices of pizza and bottles of beer:

Slices of Pizza	Marginal Utility	Bottles of Beer	Marginal Utility
1	100	1	60
2	80	2	50
3	60	3	30
4	50	4	20

If Allen maximizes his total utility by consuming 3 slices of pizza and 3 bottles of beer, which one of the following is the ratio of the price of a slice of pizza to the price of a bottle of beer?

   A. 1:1
   B. 1:2
   C. 2:1
   D. 2:2

Inputs and the Cost of Production

aq.micro.input.csts.001_2017

88. In the long run, a firm may experience increasing returns due to

   A. The law of diminishing returns.
   B. Opportunity costs.
   C. Comparative advantage.
   D. Economies of scale.

AICPA.040115BEC-SIM

89. Which one of the following cost curves does not have a general "U-shape"?

   A. Average variable cost (AVC) curve.
   B. Average fixed cost (AFC) curve.
   C. Average total cost (ATC) curve.
   D. Marginal cost (MC) curve.

AICPA.040116BEC-SIM

90. In the long run, if all input factors to a production process are increased by 100%, but total output increases by only 75%, this indicates

   A. Increasing returns to scale.
   B. Constant returns to scale.
   C. Decreasing returns to scale.
   D. Diminishing returns.

Market Structure and Firm Strategy

Introduction to Market Structure

AICPA082257BEC.EM.I.II

91. Which one of the following is central to determining the nature of market structure in a free-market economy?

    A. The size of the market.
    B. The nature of the good or service provided by the market.
    C. The extent of competition in the market.
    D. Whether the market provides goods or, alternatively, services.

AICPA082268BEC.EM.I.II

92. Which of the following is not one of the four common market structures used in economic analysis in a free-market economy?

    A. Perfect competition.
    B. Socialism.
    C. Oligopoly.
    D. Perfect monopoly.

Perfect Competition

AICPA.090499BEC-SIM

93. In the short run, a firm in perfect competition will cease to produce when which of the following conditions exists?

    A. Price is less than average variable cost.
    B. Price is less than average total cost, but greater than average variable cost.
    C. Marginal revenue is less than average total cost, but greater than average variable cost.
    D. Marginal revenue is greater than average total cost.

AICPA.101113BEC

94. Which of the following is assumed in a perfectly competitive financial market?

    A. No single trader or traders can have a significant impact on market prices.
    B. Some traders can impact market prices more than others.
    C. Trading prices vary based on supply only.
    D. Information about borrowing/lending activities is only available to those willing to pay market prices.

Perfect Monopoly

AICPA.090501BEC-SIM

95. In the long run, when a monopolistic firm produces at the quantity that maximizes revenue, will the firm use resources efficiently or inefficiently and will its price be higher or lower than in a competitive environment?

	Use of Resources	Monopoly Price
A.	Efficient	Higher than perfect competition
B.	Inefficient	Lower than perfect competition
C.	Efficient	Lower than perfect competition
D.	Inefficient	Higher than perfect competition

AICPA.090502BEC-SIM

96. In a perfect monopoly market structure, which of the following is characteristic of a natural monopoly?

    A. A firm has control of an essential input to the production process.
    B. A firm has increasing returns to scale.
    C. A firm owns a secret formula.
    D. A firm has a government-granted exclusive franchise.

Monopolistic Competition

assess.AICPA.BEC.mktstrct.mnpl.comp-0021

97. Which of the following statements is correct regarding the variety and price of products produced under monopolistic competition as compared to production under perfect competition?

    A. The monopolistically competitive industry produces a greater variety of products at a lower cost per unit.
    B. The monopolistically competitive industry produces a greater variety of products at a higher cost per unit.
    C. The monopolistically competitive industry produces a smaller variety of products at a lower cost per unit.
    D. The monopolistically competitive industry produces a smaller variety of products at a higher cost per unit.

AICPA0811630BEC.EM.I.II

98. Which one of the following statements concerning economic profit is true for a firm in a monopolistic competitive market?

A firm in monopolistic competition can make an economic profit in the short run and/or in the long run.

	Short Run	Long Run
A.	Yes	Yes
B.	Yes	No
C.	No	Yes
D.	No	No

AICPA082258BEC.EM.I.II

99. The demand curve facing a firm in monopolistic competition is

A. Negatively sloped.
B. Positively sloped.
C. Horizontal.
D. Vertical.

Oligopoly

aq.mktstrct.olig.001_2017

100. Oligopolistic firms are less likely to collude when

A. The firms' costs structures are more similar.
B. There are fewer firms in the industry.
C. General economic conditions are recessionary.
D. The firms' products are standardized.

AICPA.130700BEC

101. Which of the following pricing policies results in establishment of a price to external customers higher than the competitive price for a given industry?

A. Collusive pricing.
B. Dual pricing.
C. Predatory pricing.
D. Transfer pricing.

Summary of Market Structure

AICPA.040128BEC-SIM

102. Which of the following market structures is least likely to be found in any industry in the U.S.?

A. Perfect competition.
B. Monopolistic competition.
C. Oligopoly.
D. Monopoly.

assess.AICPA.BEC.mktstrct.smmry-0013

103. Price discrimination is accomplished most effectively in markets with which of the following characteristics?

A. Fairly distinct segments of customers.
B. High competition that generates many price changes.
C. Advanced technology capabilities that determine optimal pricing.
D. Excess capacity that meets high demand at different price levels.

Macroeconomics

Introduction to Macroeconomics

AICPA.101233BEC-SIM

104. Which of the following issues is least likely to be relevant to the study of macroeconomics?

A. Business cycles.
B. Aggregate supply.
C. Elasticity of demand.
D. Inflation and deflation.

AICPA.101237BEC-SIM

105. In a macroeconomic free-market flow model, which of the following would be considered leakages?

	Savings	Taxes
A.	Yes	Yes
B.	Yes	No
C.	No	Yes
D.	No	No

AICPA.101238BEC-SIM

106. In a macroeconomic free-market flow model, which one of the following would not be considered an "injection"?

A. Government spending.
B. Investment spending.
C. Government subsidies.
D. Imports.

Aggregate Demand

aq.macro.agdem.001_2017

107. An individual receives an income of $3,000 per month and spends $2,500. The individual receives an increase in income of $500 per month and spends $2,800 of the total income. The individual's marginal propensity to save is

    A. 0.2.
    B. 0.4.
    C. 0.6.
    D. 0.8.

AICPA.130702BEC

108. The full-employment gross domestic product is $1.3 trillion, and the actual gross domestic product is $1.2 trillion. The marginal propensity to consume is 0.8. When inflation is ignored, what increase in government expenditures is necessary to produce full employment?

    A. $100 billion
    B. $80 billion
    C. $20 billion
    D. $10 billion

assess.AICPA.BEC.macro.agdem-0012

109. An increasing federal deficit implies which of the following conditions?

    A. Increased tax revenues and decreased entitlement payments.
    B. Decreased tax revenues and increased entitlement payments.
    C. The United States is importing more than it is exporting.
    D. The economy is in an inflationary phase.

Aggregate Supply

AICPA.090518BEC-SIM

110. The war in Iraq substantially reduced the working population, as well as other economic resources, of that country. Which one of the following most likely occurred in the Iraqi economy as a result of the reduced working population?

    A. The aggregate demand curve shifted outward.
    B. The aggregate supply curve shifted outward.
    C. The aggregate supply curve shifted inward.
    D. The aggregate supply curve will remain unchanged.

AICPA.090519BEC-SIM

111. An increase in the minimum wage rate would likely result in which one of the following?

    A. The aggregate supply curve would shift outward.
    B. The aggregate supply curve would shift inward.
    C. The aggregate supply curve would remain unchanged.
    D. The quantity supplied at various prices will increase.

AICPA082263BEC.EM.II.I

112. Which of the following effects is most likely to accompany an unexpected reduction in aggregate supply, assuming a conventional supply curve?

    A. An increase in the price level.
    B. A decrease in the price level.
    C. A decrease in the rate of unemployment.
    D. An increase in the gross domestic product (GDP).

Aggregate (Economy) Equilibrium

AICPA.090520BEC-SIM

113. The aggregate demand and aggregate supply curves intersect at a price and quantity that are

    A. At (equal to) potential GDP.
    B. Above potential GDP.
    C. Below potential GDP.
    D. Either at, above, or below potential GDP.

AICPA.090522BEC-SIM

114. An increase in the value of the Chinese currency (the RMB) relative to the U.S. dollar would most likely cause which of the following?

    A. Increased aggregate demand in the U.S.
    B. Increased aggregate supply in the U.S.
    C. Increase aggregate demand in China.
    D. Decrease aggregate supply in China.

AICPA0811632BEC.II.C

115. Assume increased capital investment results in higher levels of output of goods, but demand remains unchanged. What will be the likely effect on aggregate equilibrium quantity and price if a conventional supply curve is assumed?

	Quantity	Price
A.	Increase	Increase
B.	Increase	Decrease
C.	Decrease	Increase
D.	Decrease	Decrease

AICPA0811634BEC.II.C

116. Assume increased capital investment results in higher levels of output of goods, but demand remains unchanged. What will be the likely effect on aggregate equilibrium quantity and price if a Keynesian supply curve is assumed and the level of aggregate demand is at greater than full employment?

	Quantity	Price
A.	Increase	Increase
B.	Increase	Decrease
C.	Decrease	Increase
D.	Decrease	Decrease

Gross Measures—Economic Activity

aicpa.aq.macro.econact.001_17

117. Which of the following statements is correct regarding an economy at the peak of the business cycle?

    A. The economy will be in a static equilibrium.
    B. The economy will be at the natural rate of unemployment.
    C. Incomes will be stable.
    D. The rate of inflation will decrease.

AICPA.090508BEC-SIM

118. A good produced in Year 1 that was in the finished goods inventory on December 31, Year 1, and was sold in January Year 2 would be included in whole or in part in the GDP of which year(s)?

	Year 1	Year 2
A.	Yes	Yes
B.	Yes	No
C.	No	Yes
D.	No	No

AICPA.110515BEC

119. Which of the following indicates that the economy is in a recessionary phase?

    A. The rate of unemployment decreases.
    B. The purchasing power of money declines.
    C. Potential national income exceeds actual national income.
    D. There is a shortage of essential raw materials and costs are rising.

Gross Measures—Employment/ Unemployment

aq.macro.emplmt.001_2017

120. The rate of unemployment caused by changes in the composition of employment opportunities over time is referred to as the

    A. Frictional unemployment rate.
    B. Cyclical unemployment rate.
    C. Structural unemployment rate.
    D. Seasonal unemployment rate.

AICPA.101242BEC-SIM

121. There can be official full employment when there is which of the following kinds of unemployment?

    I. Structural unemployment.
    II. Frictional unemployment.
    III. Seasonal unemployment.

    A. Only I.
    B. Only II.
    C. Only III.
    D. I, II, and/or III.

AICPA.110512BEC

122. Which of the following types of unemployment typically results from technological advances?

    A. Cyclical.
    B. Frictional.
    C. Structural.
    D. Short-term.

Business Cycles and Indicators

aicpa.aq.macro.bsccle.002_2-18

123. Which of the following options describes the phases of business cycle, in order of occurrence?

    A. Recession, recovery, trough, peak
    B. Peak, recession, trough, recovery
    C. Peak, recovery, trough, recession
    D. Trough, recession, recovery, peak

AICPA.061270BEC-BEC.II

124. Which of the following segments of the economy will be least affected by the business cycle?

    A. Commercial construction industry.
    B. Machinery and equipment industry.
    C. Residential construction industry.
    D. Healthcare industry.

AICPA.110504BEC

125. Variations between business cycles are most likely attributable to which of the following factors?

   A. The law of diminishing returns.
   B. Comparative advantage.
   C. Duration and intensity.
   D. Opportunity costs.

Price Levels and Inflation/Deflation

aicpa.aq.macro.pricelev.002_17

126. The consensus of economic forecasts indicates that consumer prices are likely to increase because of increases in aggregate demand. Which of the following outcomes is most likely to occur as prices increase?

   A. Quantity of output increases if there is capacity to produce.
   B. Unemployment increases.
   C. Profits fall if all costs are fixed.
   D. Profits rise even if cost increase.

aq.macro.pricelev.001_2017

127. A lender and a borrower signed a contract for a $1,000 loan for one year. The lender asked the borrower to pay 3% interest. Inflation occurred and prices rose by 2% over the next year. At the end of the year, the borrower repaid $1,030 (principal + interest). What is the amount worth in real terms (i.e., after inflation)?

   A. $1,060.90.
   B. $1,050.60.
   C. $1,029.41.
   D. $1,009.80.

AICPA.120637BEC

128. The controller of Gray, Inc. has decided to use ratio analysis to analyze business cycles for the past two years in an effort to identify seasonal patterns. Which of the following formulas should be used to compute percentage changes for account balances for year 1 to year 2?

   A. (Prior balance – current balance) / current balance.
   B. (Prior balance – current balance) / prior balance.
   C. (Current balance – prior balance) / current balance.
   D. (Current balance – prior balance) / prior balance.

AICPA.120639BEC

129. How does inflation distort reported income?

   A. Wages are NOT reflective of current labor rates.
   B. Sales are NOT reflective of current product prices.
   C. Depreciation is NOT reflective of current fixed-asset replacement costs.
   D. Interest expense is NOT reflective of current borrowing rates.

Money, Banking, and Monetary/Fiscal Policy

aicpa.aq.macro.money.003_17

130. A country reduces its rate of monetary growth. Which of the following is the expected result for the country's economy?

   A. Higher net exports
   B. Higher investment
   C. Lower GDP growth
   D. Lower interest rates

AICPA.082036BEC-2.C

131. Which of the following strategies would the Federal Reserve most likely pursue under an expansionary policy?

   A. Purchase federal securities and lower the discount rate.
   B. Reduce the reserve requirement while raising the discount rate.
   C. Raise the reserve requirement and lower the discount rate.
   D. Raise the reserve requirement and raise the discount rate.

AICPA.090803.BEC

132. Which of the following Federal Reserve policies would increase money supply?

   A. Change the multiplier effect.
   B. Increase the reserve requirement.
   C. Reduce the discount rate.
   D. Sell more U.S. Treasury bonds.

International Economics

Introduction and Reasons for International Activity

aicpa.aq.reasn.intnl.001_17

133. In which of the following situations would it be advantageous for a country to export a manufactured product?

    A. The country's government prefers to be self-sufficient.
    B. The country has an absolute advantage in the production of a complementary product.
    C. The country has a comparative advantage in the production of the item.
    D. The country has a higher opportunity cost for production of the item.

AICPA.090523BEC-SIM

134. Which of the following typically is not a reason for international economic activity by a U.S. entity?

    A. Market diversification.
    B. Resource acquisition.
    C. Protection of domestic manufacturing capabilities.
    D. Reduce production costs.

AICPA.090525BEC-SIM

135. The concept of comparative advantage in international business activity is based on which one of the following?

    A. Differences in relative absolute costs.
    B. Law of diminishing returns.
    C. Differences in relative opportunity costs.
    D. Differences in relative cost of labor.

Issues at the National Level

aicpa.aq.iss.ntn.lvl.003_2-18

136. Information regarding four aluminum manufacturers is as follows:

	Alpha Co.	Brighton Co.	Cobalt Co.	Driftwood Co.
Average production cost	$60	$54	$53	$52
Mill price to domestic customers	56	49	54	49
Mill price to foreign customers	59	57	55	55
Spot aluminum price	56	56	56	56

According to international law, which of the following aluminum producers is dumping?

    A. Alpha
    B. Brighton
    C. Cobalt
    D. Driftwood

aicpa.aq.iss.ntnl.lvl.001_17

137. Which of the following items represents a reduction in the balance of payment accounts for the United States?

    A. Exports of services to residents of foreign nations
    B. Loans to domestic entities by foreign commercial banks.
    C. Foreign purchases of assets in the United States
    D. Import of assets from foreign countries

aicpa.aq.iss.ntnl.lvl.002_17

138. Which of the following is the most likely result of imposing tariffs to increase domestic employment?

    A. A long-run reallocation of workers from export industries to protected domestic industries
    B. A short-run increase in domestic employment in import industries from export industries
    C. A decrease in tariff rates of foreign nations
    D. A decrease in consumer prices in the domestic market

AICPA.040145BEC-SIM

139. Which of the following is not an account used by the U.S. to account for transactions and balances with other nations (i.e., those not in the U.S. balance of payments statement)?

    A. Current account.
    B. Non-current account.
    C. Capital account.
    D. Financial account.

Role of Exchange Rates

aq.rlexchg.rts.004_2017

140. Assuming that the real rate of interest is the same in both countries, if Country A has a higher nominal interest rate than Country B, then the currency of Country A will likely be selling at a

    A. Forward discount relative to the currency of Country B.
    B. Forward premium relative to the currency of Country B.
    C. Spot discount relative to the currency of Country B.
    D. Spot premium relative to the currency of Country B.

aq.rlexchg.rts.003_2017

141. Generally, exchange rates are determined by

    A. Each industrial country's government.
    B. The International Monetary Fund.
    C. Supply and demand in the foreign exchange market.
    D. Exporters and importers of manufactured goods.

AICPA.090804.BEC

142. Freely fluctuating exchange rates perform which of the following functions?

    A. They automatically correct a lack of equilibrium in the balance of payments.
    B. They make imports cheaper and exports more expensive.
    C. They impose constraints on the domestic economy.
    D. They eliminate the need for foreign currency hedging.

Issues at Entity Level

Currency Exchange Rate Issue

aicpa.aq.curr.exchng.rtiss.003_17

143. A U.S.-based company decides to invest capital in an emerging market operation that has a lower expected return rate compared to the expected return for an alternative domestic operation. Which of the following statements correctly supports this decision?

    A. Management expects the U.S. dollar to decline in value relative to the foreign location's currency.
    B. Management expects inflation to increase in the emerging market compared to the U.S. inflation rate.
    C. Management expects inflation to decrease in the U.S. compared to the foreign location's inflation rate.
    D. Management expects the U.S. dollar to strengthen in value relative to the foreign location's currency.

aicpa.aq.curr.exchng.rtiss.004_17

144. A company considers investing $20 million in a foreign company whose local currency is under pressure. The company suspects that the exchange rate may fluctuate soon. The exchange rate at the time of the investment is 2.57 to $1.00. After the investment, the exchange rate changes to 3.15 to $1.00. What is the change in the value of the company's investment in U.S. dollars?

    A. 18.4% increase.
    B. 18.4% decrease.
    C. 22.6% increase.
    D. 22.6% decrease.

aq.curr.exchng.rtiss.002_2017

145. An American importer expects to pay a British supplier £500,000 in three months. Which of the following hedges is **best** for the importer to fix the price in dollars?

    A. Buying British pound call options.
    B. Buying British pound put options.
    C. Selling British pound put options.
    D. Selling British pound call options.

International Transfer Price Issue

aq.trans.prciss.001_2017

146. A multinational company operates a production facility in Country A and a distribution outlet in Country B. The tax rates are 40% in Country A and 50% in Country B. The production facility sells the goods to the distribution outlet, both of which are wholly owned by the multinational company. The internal sale of goods occurs at a "transfer" price set by the multinational company. Assuming no nontax considerations and no interference from the tax authorities of the two countries, the company should

    A. Maximize the transfer price.
    B. Minimize the transfer price.
    C. Establish a transfer price that results in the same profit margin for both operations.
    D. Use a transfer price based on the market price for the product that other producers charge.

AICPA.090528BEC-SIM

147. Which of the following best describes "transfer pricing?"

   A. The cost to convert financial statements from one country's currency to another country's currency.
   B. The amount of sales denominated in a foreign currency.
   C. The determination of the amounts at which transactions between affiliated entities will be recorded.
   D. The amount of taxes paid on amounts earned in foreign countries.

AICPA.101256BEC-SIM

148. Which of the following is not a common basis for establishing a transfer price between affiliated entities?

   A. Costs incurred by the selling affiliate.
   B. Costs incurred by the buying affiliate.
   C. Fair value based on the price in the market.
   D. Price negotiated between affiliates.

Globalization

Introduction to Globalization

AICPA.101121BEC-SIM

149. Which one of the following international organizations has the promotion of economic development through loans to developing countries as a primary purpose?

   A. International Monetary Fund (IMF).
   B. World Bank.
   C. World Trade Organization (WTO).
   D. United Nations (UN).

AICPA.101123BEC-SIM

150. Which one of the following would not be a purpose of the General Agreement on Tariffs and Trade (GATT)?

   A. Eliminating import quotas.
   B. Harmonizing intellectual property laws.
   C. Eliminating subsidies to export industries.
   D. Establishing procedures for collection of international debt.

AICPA.101125BEC-SIM

151. Foreign direct investment occurs when a domestic entity invests in

	Foreign Bonds	**Foreign Production Facilities**
A.	Yes	Yes
B.	Yes	No
C.	No	Yes
D.	No	No

Globalization of Trade

AICPA.101126BEC-SIM

152. Which of the following statements regarding international trade is/are correct?

   I. International trade has been facilitated by regional trade agreements.
   II. International trade benefits both exporters and importers.

   A. I only.
   B. II only.
   C. Both I and II.
   D. Neither I nor II.

AICPA.101128BEC-SIM

153. Which of the following enters into the determination of gross domestic product of a country?

	Imports	**Exports**
A.	Yes	Yes
B.	Yes	No
C.	No	Yes
D.	No	No

AICPA.101132BEC-SIM

154. Which of the following countries is the world's largest exporter of goods/services?

   A. China.
   B. Germany.
   C. Japan.
   D. U.S.

Globalization of Production

AICPA.101136BEC-SIM

155. Outsourcing of goods may involve acquisition of

	Raw Materials	**Final Goods**
A.	Yes	Yes
B.	Yes	No
C.	No	Yes
D.	No	No

AICPA.101138BEC-SIM

156. Which of the following is least likely to be a risk encountered when goods are outsourced to a foreign supplier and payment is denominated in the foreign supplier's currency?

    A. Quality risk.
    B. Security risk.
    C. Market risk.
    D. Currency exchange risk.

AICPA.101140BEC-SIM

157. Which of the following, if either, would serve to mitigate risks associated with outsourcing?

    I. Negotiate for payment to the foreign supplier be made in the foreign currency.
    II. Include an arbitration clause in the contract with the foreign supplier.

    A. I only.
    B. II only.
    C. Both I and II.
    D. Neither I nor II.

Globalization of Capital Markets

AICPA.101141BEC-SIM

158. Capital markets facilitate the trading of

	Stocks	Bonds
A.	Yes	Yes
B.	Yes	No
C.	No	Yes
D.	No	No

AICPA.101146BEC-SIM

159. In which of the following circumstances, as the dollar changes against the foreign currency, would an investment in a foreign currency result in fewer dollars and a borrowing in a foreign currency cost more dollars?

	Investment in Foreign Currency	Borrowing in Foreign Currency
A.	Dollar weakens	Dollar weakens
B.	Dollar weakens	Dollar strengthens
C.	Dollar strengthens	Dollar weakens
D.	Dollar strengthens	Dollar strengthens

Globalization and Power Shifts

aq.glob.pwrsfts.001_2017

160. Which of the following countries has **not** experienced a decline in share of worldwide output over the past approximately 40 years?

    A. U.S.
    B. Japan
    C. Brazil
    D. Germany

AICPA.101152BEC-SIM

161. Which one of the following countries is not one of the world's largest exporters of goods and services?

    A. Germany.
    B. Mexico.
    C. U.S.
    D. China.

AICPA.101154BEC-SIM

162. Which one of the following is most likely the U.S. share of worldwide exports?

    A. 50%.
    B. 15%.
    C. 10%.
    D. 2%.

Becoming Global

aq.bec.glob.002_2017

163. A company can reduce the potential loss from host-government expropriation of a foreign subsidiary by

    A. Financing the subsidiary with local-country capital.
    B. Structuring operations so that the subsidiary has value as a stand-alone company.
    C. Reducing the cost of capital to reflect political risk when assessing foreign investment opportunities.
    D. Selling products in the local country.

AICPA.101183BEC-SIM

164. Government-imposed trade barriers may restrict

	Imports	Exports
A.	Yes	Yes
B.	Yes	No
C.	No	Yes
D.	No	No

AICPA.101186BEC-SIM

165. Which one of the following forms of international business is most likely to give an entity the greatest control over an international business activity?

    A. Foreign joint venture.
    B. Foreign licensing agreement.
    C. Foreign franchising agreement.
    D. Foreign subsidiary.

AICPA.101187BEC-SIM

166. Which one of the following is least likely an advantage associated with the acquisition of a pre-existing foreign entity?

    A. It may block competition from entering the foreign market in which the acquired entity operates.
    B. Provides quicker entry into a market than developing a new entity in the foreign market.
    C. Assures synergies between the acquiring entity and the acquired entity.
    D. Provides historical financial information that is useful to the acquiring entity.

Business Strategy and Market Analysis

Introduction to Business Strategy and Market Analysis

AICPA.101069BEC-SIM

167. Which of the following is not a generic strategy identified by Michael Porter?

    A. Focus.
    B. Cost leadership.
    C. First-to-market.
    D. Differentiation.

AICPA.101070BEC-SIM

168. The measurement of post-performance characteristics is most likely to be associated with which one of the following activities of the strategic planning process?

    A. Environmental analysis.
    B. Evaluation and control.
    C. Formulating strategy.
    D. Establishing objectives.

AICPA.101071BEC-SIM

169. Which of the following identifies a framework for gauging the attractiveness of the competitive environment of an industry?

    A. Five forces.
    B. SWOT.
    C. PEST.
    D. Focus.

Macro-Environmental Analysis

AICPA.101079BEC-SIM

170. PEST is an acronym for

    A. Political, Environmental, Social, and Technological.
    B. Policy, Environmental, Social, and Technological.
    C. Political, Economic, Social, and Technological.
    D. Policy, Economic, Social, and Technological.

AICPA.101080BEC-SIM

171. In the context of PEST analysis, the analysis of labor law would be most likely to fall under which of the PEST categories?

    A. Political.
    B. Economic.
    C. Social.
    D. Technological.

AICPA.101082BEC-SIM

172. Which of the following factors is explicitly included in PESTEL analysis but is not explicitly in PEST analysis?

    A. Economic growth rate.
    B. Level of research and development.
    C. Political stability.
    D. Climate conditions.

Industry Analysis

AICPA.101086BEC-SIM

173. Which one of the following features would not create a higher level of competitive threat posed by substitute goods or services in an industry?

    A. Prices of substitutes are low relative to the price of an entity's goods or services.
    B. Substitutes are readily available.
    C. Low cost to buyers to switch goods/services.
    D. Customers have strong brand loyalty.

AICPA.101087BEC-SIM

174. In which one of the following circumstances are customers most likely to have the greatest ability to affect product prices?

    A. There are few suppliers of the product.
    B. There are many unrelated, low-quantity buyers of the product.
    C. Information about the sources of the product is widely available.
    D. The product is highly specialized.

AICPA.101088BEC-SIM

175. Which one of the following sets of characteristics should have the highest intensity of rivalry within an industry?

	Industry Fixed Cost Structure	Degree of Product Differentiation
A.	High	High
B.	Low	High
C.	High	Low
D.	Low	Low

Entity/Environment Relationship Analysis

AICPA.101099BEC-SIM

176. A regulatory agency has been considering the imposition of stricter regulations on an industry. Under SWOT analysis, the possibility of this new regulation would be considered

A. a strength.
B. a threat.
C. a weakness.
D. an opportunity.

AICPA.101100BEC-SIM

177. Which one of the following would be least likely to be a possible threat to an entity?

A. The possibility of changes in customer preferences.
B. The prospect of new regulations on an entity's industry.
C. Decreases in international trade barriers.
D. The possibility of restricted access to needed natural resources.

AICPA.101101BEC-SIM

178. Which of the following SWOT matrix relationship categories (intersections) poses the greatest risk to an entity?

A. S/O.
B. S/T.
C. W/T.
D. W/O.

Generic Strategies

AICPA.101089BEC-SIM

179. Which one of the following is not a generic strategy identified by Porter?

A. Market focus.
B. Cost leadership.
C. Market monopoly.
D. Differentiation.

AICPA.101091BEC-SIM

180. Which of the following is a characteristic of a cost leadership entity?

	Significant Capital Invested	Efficient Distribution
A.	No	No
B.	No	Yes
C.	Yes	No
D.	Yes	Yes

AICPA.101092BEC-SIM

181. Under which of the following strategies, if either, would the strength and dedication of an entity's marketing function be critical?

	Cost Leadership	Differentiation
A.	Yes	Yes
B.	Yes	No
C.	No	Yes
D.	No	No

Summary and Extensions

AICPA.101075BEC-SIM

182. Goals established in the strategic planning process should be

	Measurable	Time-bound
A.	Yes	Yes
B.	Yes	No
C.	No	Yes
D.	No	No

AICPA.101076BEC-SIM

183. PEST analysis and SWOT analysis are assessment techniques used in the strategic planning process. Are these forms of analysis primarily concerned with "where" an entity should be located or with "how" an entity should operate?

	PEST Analysis	SWOT Analysis
A.	How	Where
B.	How	How
C.	Where	How
D.	Where	Where

Financial Management

Introduction to Financial Management

Concepts and Tools

Cost Concepts

AICPA.110508BEC

184. The ABC Company is trying to decide between keeping an existing machine and replacing it with a new machine. The old machine was purchased just two years ago for $50,000 and had an expected life of 10 years. It now costs $1,000 a month for maintenance and repairs, due to a mechanical problem. A new replacement machine is being considered, with a cost of $60,000. The new machine is more efficient and it will only cost $200 a month for maintenance and repairs. The new machine has an expected life of 10 years. In deciding to replace the old machine, which of the following factors, ignoring income taxes, should ABC **not** consider?

   A. Any estimated salvage value on the old machine.
   B. The original cost of the old machine.
   C. The estimated life of the new machine.
   D. The lower maintenance cost of the new machine.

AICPA.120627BEC

185. Management at MDK Corp. is deciding whether to replace a delivery van. A new delivery van costing $40,000 can be purchased to replace the existing delivery van, which cost the company $30,000 and has accumulated depreciation of $20,000. An employee of MDK has offered $12,000 for the old delivery van. Ignoring income taxes, which of the following correctly states relevant costs when making the decision whether to replace the delivery vehicle?

   A. Purchase price of new van, disposal price of old van, gain on sale of old van.
   B. Purchase price of new van, purchase price of old van, gain on sale of old van.
   C. Purchase price of new van, disposal price of old van.
   D. Purchase price of new van, purchase price of old van, accumulated depreciation of old van, gain on sale of old van, disposal price of old van.

AICPA.120630BEC

186. A company uses its company-wide cost of capital to evaluate new capital investments. What is the implication of this policy when the company has multiple operating divisions, each having unique risk attributes and capital costs?

   A. High-risk divisions will over-invest in new projects and low-risk divisions will under-invest in new projects.
   B. High-risk divisions will under-invest in high-risk projects.
   C. Low-risk divisions will over-invest in low-risk projects.
   D. Low-risk divisions will over-invest in new projects and high-risk divisions will under-invest in new projects.

assess.AICPA.BEC.cst.cncpts-0023

187. A company had a choice between project X and project Y. The net present value of project X is $1,000,000, and the net present value of project Y is $750,000. The company chose project X. What is the opportunity cost of that decision?

   A. $250,000
   B. $750,000
   C. $1,000,000
   D. $1,750,000

Time Value of Money Tools

AICPA.082046BEC-III.A

188. Which of the following changes would result in the highest present value?

   A. A $100 decrease in taxes each year for four years.
   B. A $100 decrease in the cash outflow each year for three years.
   C. A $100 increase in disposal value at the end of four years.
   D. A $100 increase in cash inflows each year for three years.

AICPA.950538BEC-AR

189. Pole Co. is investing in a machine with a 3-year life. The machine is expected to reduce annual cash operating costs by $30,000 in each of the first 2 years and by $20,000 in year 3. Present values of an annuity of $1 at 14% are:

Period	1	0.88
	2	1.65
	3	2.32

Using a 14% cost of capital, what is the present value of these future savings?

A. $59,600
B. $60,800
C. $62,900
D. $69,500

assess.AICPA.BEC.tmval.mnytls-0024

190. An individual received an inheritance from a grandparent's estate. The money can be invested and the individual can either (a) receive a $20,000 lump-sum amount at the end of 10 years or (b) receive $1,400 at the end of each year for the next 10 years. The individual wants a rate of return of 12% and uses the following information:

Present value of $1 = 0.322
Present value of annuity of $1 = 5.650.

What is the preferred investment option and what is its net present value?

A. Option b, $451.
B. Option a, $6,440.
C. Option b, $7,910.
D. Option a, $113,000.

Interest Rate Concepts and Calculations

aq.int.rtscncpts.001_2017

191. Which one of the following describes the relationship shown by a yield curve?

A. A yield curve shows the relationship between liquidity and bond interest rates.
B. A yield curve shows the relationship between time to maturity and bond interest rates.
C. A yield curve shows the relationship between risk and bond interest rates.
D. A yield curve shows the relationship between bond interest rates and bond prices.

AICPA.110510BEC

192. A corporation obtains a loan of $200,000 at an annual rate of 12%. The corporation must keep a compensating balance of 20% of any amount borrowed on deposit at the bank, but it normally does not have a cash balance account with the bank. What is the effective cost of the loan?

A. 12.0%
B. 13.3%
C. 15.0%
D. 16.0%

AICPA.120635BEC

193. The following information is available on market interest rates:

The risk-free rate of interest	2%
Inflation premium	1%
Default risk premium	3%
Liquidity premium	2%
Maturity risk premium	1%

What is the market rate of interest on a one-year U.S. Treasury bill?

A. 3%.
B. 5%.
C. 6%.
D. 7%.

assess.AICPA.BEC.int.rtscncpts-0025

194. A company wants to approximate the 12% annual interest rate based on a 365-day year it pays on its working capital loan. Which of the following terms should the company offer its customers?

A. 2.00%, 15, net 45.
B. 1.00%, 15, net 45.
C. 0.75%, 10, net 30.
D. 0.50%, 10, net 30.

Financial Valuation

Introduction to Financial Valuation

AICPA.101177BEC-SIM

195. Which of the following U.S. GAAP levels of inputs for valuation purposes is/are based on observable inputs?

	Level 1	Level 2	Level 3
A.	Yes	Yes	Yes
B.	Yes	Yes	No
C.	Yes	No	No
D.	No	No	Yes

AICPA.101178BEC-SIM

196. Which one of the following U.S. GAAP approaches to determining fair value converts future amounts to current amounts?

    A. Market approach.
    B. Sales comparison approach.
    C. Income approach.
    D. Cost approach.

AICPA.101179BEC-SIM

197. Conceptually, which one of the following U.S. GAAP approaches for determining value is most likely to provide the best evidence of fair value?

    A. Market approach.
    B. Income approach.
    C. Correlation approach.
    D. Cost approach.

Valuation Techniques—General

AICPA.101191BEC-SIM

198. Assuming they are traded in an active market, which of the following types of investments, if any, could be valued using level 1 inputs of the U.S. GAAP hierarchy of inputs for determining fair value?

	Equity Securities	Debt Securities
A.	Yes	Yes
B.	Yes	No
C.	No	Yes
D.	No	No

AICPA.101193BEC-SIM

199. Which of the following levels of the U.S. GAAP hierarchy of inputs used for determining fair value can be based on inputs not directly observable for the item being valued?

	Level 1	Level 2	Level 3
A.	Yes	Yes	Yes
B.	Yes	Yes	No
C.	Yes	No	Yes
D.	No	Yes	Yes

AICPA.101194BEC-SIM

200. Quoted prices in which of the following types of markets could be level 2 inputs in determining fair value under the U.S. GAAP hierarchy of inputs for fair value determination?

	Active Markets	Inactive Markets
A.	Yes	Yes
B.	Yes	No
C.	No	Yes
D.	No	No

Valuation Techniques—CAPM

aicpa.aq.valtech.capm.001_17

201. What does beta measure in the capital asset pricing model?

    A. The volatility of a stock relative to its competitors
    B. The volatility of a stock relative to the market
    C. The additional return required over the risk-free rate
    D. Unsystematic risk

aq.bec.valtech.capm.001_2017

202. Which of the following categories of risk does an investment's beta measure?

    A. The investment's systematic risk.
    B. The investment's unsystematic risk.
    C. The investment's default risk.
    D. The investment's interest rate risk.

AICPA.101200BEC-SIM

203. Which one of the following is not a limitation of the capital asset pricing model?

    A. It assumes that there are no restrictions on borrowing at the risk-free rate of return.
    B. It assumes that no external costs are associated with the investment.
    C. It fails to consider the time value of money.
    D. It fails to consider risk derived from other than variances from the asset class benchmark.

Valuation Techniques—Option Pricing

AICPA.101203BEC-SIM

204. Which one of the following is not a limitation of the basic Black-Scholes option pricing model?

    A. It fails to consider the probability that the option will be exercised.
    B. It assumes the stock does not pay dividends.
    C. It assumes the risk-free rate of return used for discounting remains constant during the option period.
    D. It assumes the option can be exercised only at the expiration date.

AICPA.101204BEC-SIM

205. Which one of the following characteristics is not an advantage of the Black-Scholes option pricing model?

   A. Incorporates the probability that the price of the stock will pay off within the time to expiration.
   B. Incorporates the probability that the option will be exercised.
   C. Discounts the exercise price.
   D. Accommodates options when the price of the underlying stock changes significantly and rapidly.

AICPA.101205BEC-SIM

206. Charles Allen was granted options to buy 100 shares of Dean Company stock. The options expire in one year and have an exercise price of $60.00 per share. An analysis determines that the stock has an 80% probability of selling for $72.50 at the end of the one-year option period and a 20% probability of selling for $65.00 at the end of the year. Dean Company's cost of funds is 10%. Which one of the following is most likely the current value of the 100 stock options?

   A. $1,000
   B. $1,100
   C. $6,875
   D. $7,100

Valuation Techniques—Business Entity

AICPA.101217BEC-SIM

207. The P/E ratio for a share of common stock is computed as:

   A. Par value/EPS.
   B. Par value × EPS.
   C. EPS × Market price.
   D. Market price/EPS.

AICPA.101219BEC-SIM

208. Which one of the following approaches to valuing a business is most likely to be appropriate when the business has been losing money and is going to be sold in a distressed sale?

   A. Asset approach.
   B. Market approach.
   C. Income approach using capitalized earnings.
   D. Income approach using free cash flow.

Hedging and Derivatives

aq.bec.hedg.deriv.009_2017

209. Which of the following risks can be hedged?

	Foreign Exchange Risk	Interest Rate Risk	Default Risk
A.	Yes	Yes	No
B.	Yes	No	Yes
C.	Yes	Yes	Yes
D.	No	Yes	Yes

aq.hedg.deriv.001

210. Strobel Company has a large amount of variable rate financing due in one year. Management is concerned about the possibility of increases in short-term rates. Which one of the following would be an effective way of hedging this risk?

   A. Buy Treasury notes in the futures market.
   B. Sell Treasury notes in the futures market.
   C. Buy an option to purchase Treasury bonds.
   D. Sell an option to purchase Treasury bonds.

aq.hedg.deriv.003

211. An American importer of English clothing has contracted to pay an amount fixed in British pounds three months from now. If the importer worries that the U.S. dollar may depreciate sharply against the British pound in the interim, it would be well advised to:

   A. Buy pounds in the forward exchange market.
   B. Sell pounds in the forward exchange market.
   C. Buy dollars in the futures market.
   D. Sell dollars in the futures market.

Capital Budgeting

Introduction and Project Risk

AICPA.090538BEC-SIM

212. The presence of risk for a portfolio of projects means:

   A. More than one outcome is possible for any project.
   B. Some project will lose money.
   C. Changes in tax rates are expected to affect all projects.
   D. An inadequate number of projects is being undertaken to fully eliminate all risk.

AICPA0811602BEC.III.C

213. Which one of the following identifies the rate of return required by investors to compensate them for deferring current consumption when making an investment?

    A. Prime rate.
    B. Risk-free rate.
    C. Discount rate.
    D. Effective rate.

Evaluation Techniques

Introduction and the Payback Period Approach

AICPA.130714BEC

214. A company invested in a new machine that will generate revenues of $35,000 annually for seven years. The company will have annual operating expenses of $7,000 on the new machine. Depreciation expense, included in the operating expenses, is $4,000 per year. The expected payback period for the new machine is 5.2 years. What amount did the company pay for the new machine?

    A. $145,600
    B. $161,200
    C. $166,400
    D. $182,000

AICPA.921138BEC-P2-AR

215. Major Corp. is considering the purchase of a new machine for $5,000 that will have an estimated useful life of five years and no salvage value. The machine will increase Major's after-tax cash flow by $2,000 annually for five years. Major uses the straight-line method of depreciation and has an incremental borrowing rate of 10%. The present value factors for 10% are as follows:

Ordinary annuity with five payments	3.79
Annuity due for five payments	4.17

Using the payback method, how many years will it take to pay back Major's initial investment in the machine?

    A. 2.50
    B. 5.00
    C. 7.58
    D. 8.34

AICPA0811603BEC.III.C

216. Which one of the following approaches to capital project evaluation is primarily concerned with the relative economic ranking of projects?

    A. Net present value approach.
    B. Profitability index approach.
    C. Accounting rate of return approach.
    D. Internal rate of return approach.

Discounted Payback Period Approach

aicpa.aq.disc.pybck.001_17

217. A limitation of using the discounted payback method to evaluate a project is that it ignores which of the following?

    A. Cash flows after the payback period
    B. Duration of funds being tied up
    C. A project's cost of capital
    D. A project's break-even point

AICPA.090543BEC-SIM

218. Which one of the following is the capital budgeting evaluation approach that determines the number of periods required for the discounted cash inflows of a project to equal the discounted cash outflows?

    A. Payback period approach.
    B. Discounted payback period approach.
    C. Discounted return approach.
    D. Net present value approach.

AICPA.101120BEC

219. Which of the following statements is correct regarding the payback method as a capital budgeting technique?

    A. The payback method considers the time value of money.
    B. An advantage of the payback method is that it indicates if an investment will be profitable.
    C. The payback method provides the years needed to recoup the investment in a project.
    D. Payback is calculated by dividing the annual cash inflows by the net investment.

Accounting Rate of Return Approach

aq.bec.accrt.rtrnappr.001_2017

220. The Bread Company is planning to purchase a new machine that it will depreciate on a straight-line basis over a 10-year period. A full year's depreciation will be taken in the year of acquisition. The machine is expected to produce cash flow from operations, net of income taxes, of $3,000 in each of the 10 years. The accounting rate of return is expected to be 10% on the initial required investment. What is the cost of the new machine?

   A. $12,000
   B. $13,500
   C. $15,000
   D. $30,000

AICPA.090546BEC-SIM

221. Which of the following statements concerning the accounting rate of return approach to evaluating capital projects is/are correct?

   I. It considers the entire life of a project.
   II. It considers the time value of money.
   III. It assumes that the incremental net income is the same each year.

   A. I only.
   B. II only.
   C. I and II, only.
   D. I and III, only.

Net Present Value Approach

aq.netprs.valappr.001_2017

222. Tootco, Inc. is evaluating a new project using the net present value approach and a 12% hurdle rate. It has determined that, in addition to an investment in plant and equipment, the project will require a $12,000 investment in net working capital. The project is expected to have a 5-year life, at the end of which the investment in net working capital will be recovered. The present value of $1 and the future value of $1 factors for 5 years at 12% are 0.5674 and 1.7623, respectively.

   In carrying out its net present value analysis, how should Tootco treat the working capital requirement both when it is made at the beginning of the project and at the end of the project?

	Treatment of Working Capital Requirement	
	Beginning of Project	**End of Project**
A.	Ignore	Ignore
B.	Cash outflow of $12,000	Ignore
C.	Cash outflow of $12,000	Cash inflow of $12,000
D.	Cash outflow of $12,000	Cash inflow of $6,809

AICPA.110501BEC

223. A corporation is considering purchasing a machine that costs $100,000 and has a $20,000 salvage value. The machine will provide net annual cash inflows of $25,000 per year and has a six-year life. The corporation uses a discount rate of 10%. The discount factor for the present value of a single sum six years in the future is 0.564. The discount factor for the present value of an annuity for six years is 4.355. What is the net present value of the machine?

   A. ($2,405)
   B. $ 8,875
   C. $20,155
   D. $28,875

AICPA.130711BEC

224. A company is considering two projects, which have the following details:

	Project A	**Project B**
Expected sales	$1,000	$1,500
Cash operating expense	400	700
Depreciation	150	250
Tax rate	30%	30%

Which project would provide the largest after-tax cash inflow?

   A. Project A because after-tax cash inflow equals $465.
   B. Project A because after-tax cash inflow equals $315.
   C. Project B because after-tax cash inflow equals $635.
   D. Project B because after-tax cash inflow equals $385.

Internal Rate of Return Approach

AICPA.110503BEC

225. Which of the following metrics equates the present value of a project's expected cash inflows to the present value of the project's expected costs?

A. Net present value.
B. Return on assets.
C. Internal rate of return.
D. Economic value-added.

AICPA.120625BEC

226. Which of the following phrases defines the internal rate of return on a project?

A. The number of years it takes to recover the investment.
B. The discount rate at which the net present value of the project equals zero.
C. The discount rate at which the net present value of the project equals one.
D. The weighted-average cost of capital used to finance the project.

Project Ranking

AICPA.072957BEC-SIM

227. Which one of the following represents the formula used to calculate the profitability index for ranking projects?

A. Project Cash Flow divided by Project Cost
B. Project Cost divided by Project Cash Flow
C. Project Net Present Value divided by Project Cost
D. Project Cost divided by Project Net Present Value

AICPA.110502BEC

228. Which of the following is a limitation of the profitability index?

A. It uses free cash flows.
B. It ignores the time value of money.
C. It is inconsistent with the goal of shareholder wealth maximization.
D. It requires detailed long-term forecasts of the project's cash flows.

AICPA0811606BEC.III.B

229. Disco is considering three capital projects that have the following costs and net present values (NPV):

Project	Cost	NVP
X	$40,000	$60,000
Y	$60,000	$75,000
Z	$50,000	$30,000

Using the profitability index, which project, if any, would be ranked as the most desirable?

A. Project X.
B. Project Y.
C. Project Z.
D. None of the projects would be more desirable than the other projects.

Capital Project Ranking Decisions

aq.bec.cap.rnkng.001_2017

230. ProCo Inc. is considering a major capital undertaking. It uses the net present value approach for evaluating the economic feasibility of projects. Its prior projects are returning 12% on the amounts invested. At the time of evaluating the project being currently considered, ProCo's capital structure consisted of:

Source of Capital	Proportion of Capital Structure	After-Tax Cost of Capital
Long-term debt	60%	7.1%
Preferred stock	20%	10.5%
Common stock	20%	14.2%

What minimum hurdle (discount) rate should ProCo use in evaluating the project using the net present value approach?

A. Greater than 12.0%
B. 12.0%
C. 10.6%
D. 9.2%

aq.bec.cap.rnkng.002_2017

231. A company is considering four projects (A, B, C and D), which have the following expected cash flows:

Investment Project	Cash Outlay	Present Value of Cash Inflows
A	$1,100,000	$980,000
B	250,000	600,000
C	1,400,000	1,830,000
D	650,000	790,000

In order not to overextend its management capabilities, the company has decided to invest in only one project. If it bases its project selection on net present value (NPV), which project will the company undertake?

A. Project A.
B. Project B.
C. Project C.
D. Project D.

AICPA.130701BEC

232. Which of the following methods should be used if capital rationing needs to be considered when comparing capital projects?

A. Net present value.
B. Internal rate of return.
C. Return on investment.
D. Profitability index.

Financing Options

Introduction and Financial/Capital Structure

AICPA.070701BEC-SIM

233. Bonds Payable, which mature in 10 years, would be included as part of a firm's

	Financial Structure	Capital Structure
A.	Yes	Yes
B.	Yes	No
C.	No	Yes
D.	No	No

AICPA.090550BEC-SIM

234. The term "financial structure" refers to which one of the following?

A. All debt.
B. All equity.
C. All debt and equity.
D. All long-term debt and equity.

AICPA.090551BEC-SIM

235. Which one of the following most likely would not be considered when computing the weighted average cost of capital?

A. Short-term debt.
B. Long-term debt.
C. Common stock.
D. Preferred stock.

Short-Term (Working Capital) Financing

Introduction to Short-Term Financing

AICPA.090553BEC-SIM

236. Short-term financing is normally concerned with financing for which one of the following lengths of time?

A. Length of the operating cycle.
B. Length of the collection cycle.
C. One year or less in length.
D. Up to 10 years in length.

AICPA.090554BEC-SIM

237. Which of the following uses of accounts receivable, if either, would be considered short-term financing?

	Pledging Accounts Receivable	Factoring Accounts Receivable
A.	Yes	Yes
B.	Yes	No
C.	No	Yes
D.	No	No

Payables

aq.bec.pybls.finopt4.001_2017

238. If a firm purchases raw materials from its supplier on a 2/10, net 40, cash discount basis, the equivalent annual interest rate (using a 360-day year) of forgoing the cash discount and making payment on the 40th day is:

A. 2%
B. 18.36%
C. 24.49%
D. 36.72%

AICPA0811609BEC.III.C

239. Which one of the following forms of short-term financing is least likely to be restricted as to use of proceeds?

A. Trade accounts payable.
B. Accrued taxes payable.
C. Accrued salaries payable.
D. Short-term notes payable.

AICPA0811610BEC.III.C

240. Alpha Company borrowed $20,000 from High Bank, giving a one-year note. The terms of the note provided for 6% interest and required a 10% compensating balance. Which one of the following is the effective rate of interest on the loan?

A. 4.0%
B. 6.0%
C. 6.7%
D. 10.0%

Standby Credit and Commercial Paper

AICPA.090558BEC-SIM

241. Which one of the following is a formal legal commitment to extend credit up to some maximum amount to a borrower over a stated period?

A. Letter of credit.
B. Revolving credit agreement.
C. Line of credit.
D. Trade credit.

AICPA.090559BEC-SIM

242. Which one of the following would an importer of goods from a new foreign supplier most likely use to assure the supplier of payment?

A. Line of credit.
B. Letter of credit.
C. Trade account application.
D. Commercial paper.

Receivables and Inventory

AICPA.070704BEC-SIM

243. Po Co. plans to use its inventory as collateral for a short-term loan. Which one of the following types of loan agreements with its lender would provide Po Co. the most flexibility in the use of the inventory it pledges as collateral?

A. Field warehouse agreement.
B. Floating lien agreement.
C. Chattel mortgage agreement.
D. Terminal warehouse agreement.

AICPA.090561BEC-SIM

244. Which one of the following is a form of inventory secured loan in which the inventory is placed under the control of an independent third party?

A. Floating lien agreement.
B. Chattel mortgage agreement.
C. Field warehouse agreement.
D. Recourse loan agreement.

AICPA.090563BEC-SIM

245. Nexco, Inc. is considering factoring its accounts receivable. Factorco, Inc. has offered the following terms for accounts receivable due in 30 days:

Value of receivables to be held in reserve for contingencies	10%
Following costs are deducted at time accounts are factored:	
Interest rate on amounts provided	12%
Factor fee on total receivables factored	2%

If Nexco factors $200,000 of its accounts receivable due in 30 days with Factorco and, during that 30 days, $10,000 of those accounts receivable are reversed because the related goods were return or allowances were granted, which one of the following is the amount that Nexco will receive from Factorco at the end of the 30 day period?

A. $ -0- (no amount)
B. $ 9,800
C. $10,000
D. $19,600

Long-Term (Capital) Financing

Introduction to Long-Term Financing

AICPA08116112BEC.III.C

246. The weighted average cost of capital for a firm is determined by its cost of

	Short-term Financing	Long-term Financing
A.	Yes	Yes
B.	Yes	No
C.	No	Yes
D.	No	No

AICPA0811611BEC.III.C

247. Components of long-term financing would be part of

	Capital Structure	Financial Structure
A.	Yes	Yes
B.	Yes	No
C.	No	Yes
D.	No	No

AICPA0811613BEC.III.C

248. Which one of the following would not be considered a means of long-term financing?

A. Financial lease.
B. Common stock.
C. Trade accounts payable.
D. Bonds payable.

Long-Term Notes and Financial Leases

aq.ltnts.finlss.001_2017

249. Joe Going has arranged to become an Uber driver and will acquire a new vehicle to use strictly for that business purpose. He has the choice of either buying a new vehicle or leasing one.

If he buys a new vehicle, he would pay cash from his personal savings, which is currently earning 2% per year, not compounded. The vehicle would cost $18,000, have a 5-year life with no residual value, and generate $3,000 per year in tax-deductible depreciation at year-end. Maintenance cost of $500 would be incurred at the end of each year. Routine operating cost (gasoline, fluids, etc.) of $6,000 per year would be the responsibility of Goings and would be the same under either the buy or lease alternatives.

If Going elects to lease a vehicle, the annual tax-deductible lease expense would be $5,000 per year, payable at the beginning of each year, with the first payment due at execution of the lease. The lease would provide that the lessor be responsible for maintenance during the lease. Going's tax rate is 25%, and his cost of borrowing is 8%. The following selected present value and future value factors for 8% are available:

Present value of $1 for 5 periods	.681
Present value of an ordinary annuity for 5 periods	3.993
Present value of an annuity due for 5 periods	4.312
Future value of $1 for 5 periods	1.469
Future value of an ordinary annuity for 5 periods	5.867
Future value of an annuity due for 5 periods	6.336

Which one of the following sets indicates the method Goings should use to acquire the vehicle (purchase or lease) and most closely approximates the absolute amount of the difference between the two alternatives?

	Better Alternative	Difference between Alternatives
A.	Purchase	$7,114
B.	Purchase	$127
C.	Lease	$1,870
D.	Lease	$433

AICPA.070707BEC-SIM

250. Under which of the following described lease terms would the lessee be responsible during the term of the lease for executory costs associated with the leased asset?

	Net Lease	Net-Net Lease
A.	Yes	Yes
B.	Yes	No
C.	No	Yes
D.	No	No

AICPA.090566BEC.06

251. What would be the primary reason for a company to agree to a debt covenant limiting the percentage of its long-term debt?

A. To cause the price of the company's stock to rise.
B. To lower the company's credit rating.
C. To reduce the risk of existing debt holders.
D. To reduce the interest rate on the debt being issued.

Bonds

aq.bec.bonds7.001_2017-1

252. What would be the primary reason for a company to agree to a debt covenant on new bonds limiting the percentage of the company's long-term debt?

A. To cause the price of the company's stock to rise.
B. To lower the company's bond rating.
C. To reduce the risk for existing bondholders.
D. To reduce the interest rate on the bonds being sold.

aq.bec.bonds7.001_2017

253. The best reason corporations issue Eurobonds rather than domestic bonds is that

   A. These bonds are denominated in the currency of the country in which they are issued.
   B. These bonds are normally a less expensive form of financing because of the absence of government regulation.
   C. Foreign buyers more readily accept the issues of both large and small US corporations than do domestic investors.
   D. Eurobonds carry no foreign exchange risk.

AICPA.090568BEC-SIM

254. Which of the following statements concerning debenture bonds and secured bonds is/are correct?

   I. Debenture bonds are likely to have a greater par value than comparable secured bonds.
   II. Debenture bonds are likely to be of longer duration than comparable secured bonds.
   III. Debenture bonds are more likely to have a higher coupon rate than comparable secured bonds.

   A. I only.
   B. II only.
   C. III only.
   D. I, II, and III.

AICPA.090871BEC

255. Which of the following types of bonds is most likely to maintain a constant market value?

   A. Zero-coupon.
   B. Floating-rate.
   C. Callable.
   D. Convertible.

Preferred Stock

aicpa.aq.prfrd.stck.001_17

256. A company issued common stock and preferred stock. Projected growth rate of the common stock is 5%. The current quarterly dividend on preferred stock is $1.60. The current market price of the preferred stock is $80, and the current market price of the common stock is $95. What is the expected rate of return on the preferred stock?

   A. 2%
   B. 7%
   C. 8%
   D. 13%

AICPA.090571BEC-SIM

257. In which one of the following areas is preferred stock most likely to differ from common stock?

   A. Ownership status.
   B. Maturity date.
   C. Tax deductibility of dividends paid.
   D. Voting rights.

AICPA.090572BEC-SIM

258. Whipco has determined that its pre-tax cost of preferred stock is 12%. If its tax rate is 30%, which one of the following is its after-tax cost of preferred stock?

   A. 15.6%
   B. 12.0%
   C. 8.4%
   D. 3.6%

Common Stock

aq.bec.cmmn.stck4.001_2017

259. Which of the following statements concerning the sale of equity securities through crowdfunding are correct?

   I. Crowdfunding must take place through a SEC-registered broker-dealer or funding portal.
   II. Any company registered with the SEC may use crowdfunding.
   III. An investor is limited in the amount that can be invested through crowdfunding during a 12-month period.

   A. I only.
   B. I and II only.
   C. I and III only.
   D. I, II, and III.

aicpa.aq.cmmn.stock.004_2-18

260. A stock priced at $50 per share is expected to pay $5 in dividends and trade for $60 per share in one year. What is the expected return on this stock?

   A. 10%
   B. 20%
   C. 25%
   D. 30%

AICPA.090350BEC

261. Bander Co. is determining how to finance some long-term projects. Bander has decided it prefers the benefits of no fixed charges, no fixed maturity date, and an increase in the credit-worthiness of the company. Which of the following would best meet Bander's financing requirements?

   A. Bonds.
   B. Common stock.
   C. Long-term debt.
   D. Short-term debt.

Cost of Capital and Financing Strategies

aq.bec.cst.cap.fin.strtgy.002_2017

262. A company has $650,000 of 10% debt outstanding and $500,000 of equity financing. The required return of current equity holders is 15%, and there are no retained earnings currently available for investment purposes. If new outside equity is raised, it will cost the firm 16%. New debt would have before-tax cost of 9%, and the corporate tax rate is 50%. When calculating the marginal cost of capital, what cost should the company assign to equity capital and to the after-tax cost of debt financing?

	Cost of Equity	After-Tax Cost of Debt
A.	15%	4.5%
B.	15%	5.0%
C.	16%	4.5%
D.	16%	5.0%

AICPA.130710BEC

263. The cost of debt most frequently is measured as

   A. Actual interest rate.
   B. Actual interest rate adjusted for inflation.
   C. Actual interest rate plus a risk premium.
   D. Actual interest rate minus tax savings.

assess.AICPA.BEC.cst.cap.fin.strtgy-0026

264. Which of the following corporate characteristics would favor debt financing versus equity financing?

   A. A high tax rate.
   B. A high debt-to-equity ratio.
   C. Low aversion to risk.
   D. Below-average stock issuing costs.

Working Capital Management

Introduction to Working Capital Management

AICPA.090576BEC-SIM

265. When a financial manager takes action to minimize the firm's investment in current assets, which one of the following risks is likely to increase?

   A. Accounts receivable defaults may increase.
   B. Inventory spoilage may increase.
   C. Inventory shortages may increase.
   D. Inventory obsolescence may increase.

AICPA08116114BEC.III.C

266. Can a firm over-invest and/or under-invest in net working capital?

	Over-Invest	Under-Invest
A.	Yes	Yes
B.	Yes	No
C.	No	Yes
D.	No	No

AICPA0811615BEC.III.C

267. Which one of the following would not be considered an element of concern in working capital management?

   A. Accounts receivable.
   B. Inventory.
   C. Accounts Payable.
   D. Property, plant, and equipment.

Cash Management

aq.bec.csh.mgmt6.001_2017

268. A firm has daily cash receipts of $100,000 and collection time of 4 days. A bank has offered to reduce the collection time on the firm's deposits by 2 days using a lock-box arrangement for a monthly fee of $500. If money market rates are expected to average 6% during the year, the net annual benefit or cost from having this service is

   A. $ 3,000
   B. $12,000
   C. $0
   D. $ 6,000

AICPA.040172BEC-SIM

269. Cash management is concerned with assuring that a firm does not have:

	Too Little Cash	Too Much Cash
A.	Yes	Yes
B.	Yes	No
C.	No	Yes
D.	No	No

AICPA.040174BEC-SIM

270. Which one of the following cash management techniques focuses on cash disbursements?

A. Lock-box system.
B. Zero-balance account.
C. Pre-authorized checks.
D. Depository transfer checks.

Short-Term Securities Management

AICPA.070717BEC-SIM

271. Which of the following considerations typically would be important in selecting investments for the temporary use of "excess" cash?

	Safety of Principal	Ready Marketability
A.	Yes	Yes
B.	Yes	No
C.	No	Yes
D.	No	No

AICPA.090581BEC-SIM

272. When making short-term investments, which one of the following is the risk associated with the ability to sell an investment in a short period of time without having to make significant price concessions?

A. Purchasing power risk.
B. Interest rate risk.
C. Default risk.
D. Liquidity risk.

AICPA.090582BEC-SIM

273. Which one of the following short-term investments is likely to provide the greatest safety of principal?

A. Commercial paper.
B. Bankers' acceptance.
C. Fannie Mae securities.
D. U.S. Treasury bills.

Accounts Receivable Management

aicpa.aq.actrcvbls.mgmt.001_2-18

274. A company has credit sales of $20,000 in January, $30,000 in February, and $50,000 in March. The company collects 75% in the month of sale and 25% in the following month. The balance in accounts receivable on January 1 was $25,000. What amount is the balance in accounts receivable at closing on March 31?

A. $7,500
B. $12,500
C. $37,500
D. $45,000

AICPA.090583BEC-SIM

275. Asher Company eased its credit policy by lengthening its discount period from 10 days to 15 days. Which of the following is/are likely reasons for Asher lengthening its discount period?

I. To show a higher average age of accounts on its accounts receivable aging schedule.
II. To meet terms offered by competitors.
III. To seek to stimulate sales.

A. I only.
B. II only.
C. III only.
D. II and III, only.

AICPA.090584BEC-SIM

276. Moe's Boat Service currently does not offer a discount to encourage its customers to pay early for services provided to them. Moe has discussed with his accountant the possibility of offering a 2% discount to improve its cash conversion cycle. Moe's accountant determined the following:

Credit sales expected to remain unchanged at	$1,000,000
The 2% discount is expected to be taken on 40% of accounts receivable balance amounts.	
The average accounts receivable would likely decrease by	$30,000
Moe has an opportunity cost of 15% associated with its use of cash.	

Which one of the following is the dollar amount of net benefit or cost that Moe would obtain if the proposed 2% discount plan is implemented?

A. $ 3,500
B. $ 4,500
C. $ 8,000
D. $20,000

Inventory Management

AICPA.040187BEC-SIM

277. In computing the reorder point for an item of inventory, which of the following factors are used?

    I. Cost of inventory.
    II. Inventory usage per day.
    III. Acquisition lead-time.

    A. I and II are correct.
    B. II and III are correct.
    C. I and III are correct.
    D. I, II and III are correct.

AICPA.040188BEC-SIM

278. As a consequence of finding a more dependable supplier and adopting just-in-time inventory ordering, Dee Co. reduced its safety stock of raw materials inventory by 80%. Which one of the following would the reduction in safety stock have on Dee's economic order quantity?

    A. 80% decrease.
    B. 64% decrease.
    C. 20% increase.
    D. 0% change (no effect).

AICPA.070721BEC-SIM

279. Which of the following inventory management approaches seeks to minimize total inventory costs by considering both the restocking (reordering) cost and the carrying costs?

    A. Economic order quantity.
    B. Just-in-time.
    C. Materials requirements planning.
    D. ABC.

Current Liabilities Management

aq.bec.curr.liab.mgmt3.001_2017

280. Three suppliers offer Ruby Co. different credit terms as follows:

    Bandy Co. offers terms of 1.5/15, net 30.

    Carryl Co. offers terms of 1/10, net 30.

    Platt Co. offers terms of 2/10, net 60.

    Ruby Co. would have to borrow from a bank at an annual rate of 10% to take any cash discounts. Based on a 360-day year, which of the following options would be most attractive for Ruby Co.?

    A. Purchase from Platt Co., pay in 60 days, and do **not** borrow from the bank.
    B. Purchase from Bandy Co., pay in 15 days, and borrow from the bank.
    C. Purchase from Carryl Co., pay in 10 days, and borrow from the bank.
    D. Purchase from Bandy Co., pay in 30 days, and do **not** borrow from the bank.

AICPA.090585BEC-SIM

281. Following the hedging principle of financing, short-term liabilities would appropriately be used to finance which one of the following?

    A. The acquisition of plant machinery.
    B. The payment of bond principal at maturity.
    C. An opportunity to acquire inventory at a bargain price.
    D. The acquisition of a patent.

AICPA.090586BEC-SIM

282. In managing its working capital, your firm tries to follow the hedging principle of finance. Which one of the following would be too aggressive to be consistent with that principle as applied to working capital?

    A. Financing short-term needs with long-term funds.
    B. Financing long-term needs with short-term funds.
    C. Financing seasonal needs with short-term funds.
    D. Financing a permanent build-up in inventory with long-term debt.

Ratios and Measures for Working Capital Management

Introduction to Ratio Analysis

AICPA.090297FAR-SIM

283. Ratio analysis and related measures can be used to compare:

	A Firm Over Time	Across Firms
A.	Yes	Yes
B.	Yes	No
C.	No	Yes
D.	No	No

AICPA.090587BEC-SIM

284. Which of the following statements concerning ratio analysis is/are correct?

    I. Ratio analysis uses only monetary measures for analysis purposes.
    II. Ratio analysis uses only measures from financial statements for analysis purposes.

A. I. only.
B. II only.
C. Both I and II.
D. Neither I nor II.

AICPA.090588BEC-SIM

285. Which of the following is least likely to be a major purpose or type of ratio or measure used in financial management?

A. Solvency.
B. Operational activity.
C. Price indexes.
D. Liquidity.

Liquidity Measures

aicpa.aq.liqu.meas.001_17

286. Which of the following quantitative factors, when compared to its industry average, could be an indicator of potential corporate failure?

A. High cash flow to total liabilities
B. High retained earnings to total assets
C. High fixed cost to total cost structure
D. High fixed assets to noncurrent liabilities

AICPA.130704BEC

287. A company has income after tax of $5.4 million, interest expense of $1 million for the year, depreciation expense of $1 million, and a 40% tax rate. What is the company's times-interest-earned ratio?

A. 5.4
B. 6.4
C. 7.4
D. 10.0

AICPA.130707BEC

288. At the end of its fiscal year, Krist, Inc. had the following account balances:

Cash	$ 5,000
Accounts receivable	10,000
Inventory	20,000
Accounts payable	15,000
Short-term note payable	5,000
Long-term note payable	35,000

What is Krist's quick (acid-test) ratio?

A. 0.273
B. 0.636
C. 0.750
D. 1.750

Operational Activity Measures

aicpa.aq.oprtnl.actvt.meas.002_17

289. The main reason that a firm would strive to reduce the number of days' sales outstanding is to increase

A. Accounts receivable.
B. Cash.
C. Contribution margin.
D. Cost of goods sold.

AICPA.110519BEC-SIM

290. Cyco, Inc. determined the following concerning its operating activities:

Accounts receivable conversion cycle	18 days
Accounts payable conversion cycle	21 days
Inventory conversion cycle	24 days

Which one of the following is the length of Cyco's cash cycle?

A. 42 days.
B. 39 days.
C. 21 days.
D. 15 days.

AICPA.120626BEC

291. The following information was taken from the income statement of Hadley Co.:

Beginning inventory	17,000
Purchases	56,000
Ending inventory	13,000

What is Hadley Co.'s inventory turnover?

A. 3.
B. 4.
C. 5.
D. 6.

assess.AICPA.BEC.oprtnl.actvt.meas-0016

292. Financial information about a company is as follows:

Receivables	$ 4,000,000
Inventory	2,600,000
Payables	3,700,000
Sales	50,000,000
Cost of goods sold	45,000,000

Assuming a 365-day year, what is the number of days in the company's cash conversion cycle?

A. 18.2 days.
B. 20.3 days.
C. 21.2 days.
D. 23.5 days.

Financial Management Risk Concepts— Summary

AICPA.110507BEC

293. Which of the following types of risk can be reduced by diversification?

A. High interest rates.
B. Inflation.
C. Labor strikes.
D. Recession.

AICPA.120629BEC

294. A company has several long-term floating-rate bonds outstanding. The company's cash flows have stabilized, and the company is considering hedging interest rate risk. Which of the following derivative instruments is recommended for this purpose?

A. Structured short-term note.
B. Forward contract on a commodity.
C. Futures contract on a stock.
D. Swap agreement.

AICPA.120633BEC

295. If a CPA's client expected a high inflation rate in the future, the CPA would suggest to the client which of the following types of investments?

A. Precious metals.
B. Treasury bonds.
C. Corporate bonds.
D. Common stock.

AICPA0811627BEC.III.F

296. Which of the following, if denominated in a foreign currency, is/are subject to currency exchange risk?

	Accounts Receivable	Accounts Payable
A.	Yes	Yes
B.	Yes	No
C.	No	Yes
D.	No	No

Information Technology

Information Technology Governance

Risks and Controls in Computer-Based Accounting-Information Systems

AICPA.061218BEC-SIM

297. Morgan Property Management, Inc. recently switched from a manual accounting system to a computerized accounting system. The system supports online real-time processing in a networked environment, and six employees have been granted access to various parts of the system in order to perform their jobs. Relative to the manual system, Morgan can expect to see

A. That functions that had previously been spread across multiple employees have been combined.
B. An increase in the incidence of clerical errors.
C. A decrease in the incidence of systemic errors.
D. A decrease in the need for access controls to the accounting records.

AICPA.140501BEC-SIM

298. Checkpoint auto leasing is a small company with six employees. The best action that it can take to increase its internal control effectiveness is

A. Hire temporary employees to aid in the segregation of duties.
B. Hire a bookkeeper to perform monthly "write up" work.
C. Clearly delegate responsibilities to each employee for the functions that they are assigned.
D. Engage the owner in direct participation in the activities, including financial record-keeping, of the business.

AICPA.140502BEC-SIM

299. Which of the following statements is (are) true.

I. A greater level of control is necessary in automated than manual systems.
II. The uniformity of transaction processing is higher in automated than manual systems.

A. Both I and II.
B. I only.
C. II only.
D. Neither I or II.

The COBIT Model of IT Governance and Management

aq.it.cobit.001_17

300. The IT Steering Committee at Henry Flower's Flower Shop is determining whether the basic infrastructure of the company should include a significant component of cloud computing. In this exercise, the committee is primarily using the company's IT strategic plan to conceptually consider how cloud computing advances or detracts from the company's business objectives. In the COBIT model, this is best classified as an example of

A. Planning and Organization
B. Acquisition and Implementation
C. Delivery and Support
D. Monitoring

aicpa.aq.it.cobit.002_2-18

301. Which of the following statements is correct regarding information technology (IT) governance?

A. A primary goal of IT governance is to balance risk versus return over IT and its processes.
B. IT governance is an appropriate issue for organizations at the level of the board of directors only.
C. IT goals should be independent of strategic goals.
D. IT governance requires that the Control Objectives for Information and related Technology (COBIT) framework be adopted and implemented.

AICPA.101174BEC-SIM

302. In COBIT, the process of reviewing system response time logs falls within the _____ control process domain.

A. Acquire and implement.
B. Deliver and support.
C. Monitor and evaluate.
D. Plan and organize.

Introduction to Enterprise-Wide and Cloud-Based Systems

AICPA.120616BEC

303. A client would like to implement a management information system that integrates all functional areas within an organization to allow information exchange and collaboration among all parties involved in business operations. Which of the following systems is most effective for this application?

    A. A decision support system.
    B. An executive support system.
    C. An office automation system.
    D. An enterprise resource planning system.

AICPA.130500BEC-SIM

304. What is an example of the use of the cloud to access software and programs?

    A. IaaS
    B. PaaS
    C. SaaS
    D. SAP

AICPA.130501BEC-SIM

305. What is an example of the use of the cloud to create software and programs?

    A. IaaS
    B. PaaS
    C. SaaS
    D. SAP

IT Functions and Controls Related to People

aq.it.ctrl.ppl.001

306. Roberta is a programmer who writes applications for Parsnips Health Care. She also has access to the file library. This is a concern because she may:

    A. Grant system access inappropriately to others.
    B. Make changes in applications.
    C. Make changes to both the live and archive copies of programs.
    D. Fail to follow system change protocols.

AICPA.101243BEC

307. When a client's accounts payable computer system was relocated, the administrator provided support through a dial-up connection to a server. Subsequently, the administrator left the company. No changes were made to the accounts payable system at that time. Which of the following situations represents the greatest security risk?

    A. User passwords are not required to be in alphanumeric format.
    B. Management procedures for user accounts are not documented.
    C. User accounts are not removed upon termination of employees.
    D. Security logs are not periodically reviewed for violations.

AICPA.101251BEC

308. Which of the following information technology (IT) departmental responsibilities should be delegated to separate individuals?

    A. Network maintenance and wireless access.
    B. Data entry and antivirus management.
    C. Data entry and application programming.
    D. Data entry and quality assurance.

Role of Information and Technology in Business

IT and Business Strategy

aq.it.bus.strat.004_2017

309. A company that sells hand-carved statues from rural Indonesia online is using a _____ strategy:

    A. Digitization
    B. Product differentiation
    C. Cost leadership
    D. Integrated

aq.it.bus.strat.005_2017

310. Selling a digitized product can:

    A. Decrease its cost.
    B. Improve its quality.
    C. Both A and B.
    D. Neither A nor B.

System Types by Activity

aq.it.syst.actvty.001

311. Peetie's Pet Care has a system that examines large data sets to determine patterns in clients' use of its facilities. This is most likely an example of:

    A. Operational systems.
    B. Management information systems (MISs).
    C. Data-driven DSSs.
    D. Model-driven DSS.

AICPA.130505BEC-SIM

312. This system is most likely to include external data.

    A. Operational system.
    B. MIS.
    C. DSS.
    D. ESS.

aq.it.syst.actvty.001

313. Peetie's Pet Care has a system that examines large data sets to determine patterns in clients' use of its facilities. This is most likely an example of:

    A. Operational systems.
    B. Management information systems (MISs).
    C. Data-driven DSSs.
    D. Model-driven DSS.

System Types by Data Structure

AICPA.061223BEC-SIM

314. A specialized version of a data warehouse that contains data that is pre-configured to meet the needs of specific departments is known as

    A. A functional warehouse.
    B. A data mart.
    C. A data store.
    D. An object-oriented database.

AICPA.140506BEC-SIM

315. A data warehouse differs from a data mart because

    A. A data warehouse is more specialized than a data mart.
    B. Data mining is possible in a data mart but not a data warehouse.
    C. A data mart supports specific needs.
    D. External data is not included in a data mart.

AICPA.140507BEC-SIM

316. Which of the following statements is correct?

    I. An important advantage of flat file systems is that they are program independent.
    II. Flat file systems contain little data redundancy.

    A. Both I and II.
    B. I only.
    C. II only.
    D. Neither I or II.

Data Structures, Software, and Databases

AICPA.101053BEC-SIM

317. Database management software is considered:

    A. Outerwear.
    B. Software.
    C. Middleware
    D. B and C.

AICPA.101055BEC-SIM

318. Which of the following is not a category of computer software?

    A. System software.
    B. Programming languages.
    C. Application software.
    D. All of the above are categories of computer software.

AICPA.101261BEC

319. What is the correct ascending hierarchy of data in a system?

    A. Character, record, file, field.
    B. Field, character, file, record.
    C. Character, field, record, file.
    D. Field, record, file, character.

Information Systems Hardware

aq.intro.hrdwr.001

320. Rootin' Roberta of Sharpie Shooters Range Corp. is charged with replacing the computer used in the accounting system. She wants a quick boot time and fast access to storage. She doesn't need a lot of storage, but she wants maximum security in storage. She should consider purchasing:

    A. Computers that primary rely on optical disks.
    B. A system that primary rely on RAID storage.
    C. A system that primarily relies on cloud-based storage.
    D. Computers that primary rely on SSD storage.

AICPA.140508BEC-SIM

321. Vindaloo Corporation wants data storage for a large volume of data that is unlikely to change often. They should consider using

    A. A hard disk.
    B. Magnetic tape.
    C. CD-ROM.
    D. Memory (RAM).

IFTC-0055

322. Today organizations are using microcomputers for data presentation because microcomputer use, compared to mainframe use, is more

    A. Controllable.
    B. Conducive to data integrity.
    C. Reliable.
    D. Cost effective.

Transaction Processing

aicpa.aq.it.trans.proc.002_17

323. Real-time processing is most appropriate for which of the following bank transactions?

    A. Credit authorizations for consumer loan applicants
    B. Biweekly payroll for bank employees
    C. Purchases of fixed assets
    D. Expiration of prepaid liability insurance

aq.it.trans.proc.001

324. Simone works as an airline reservations agent. She mostly likely interacts with a:

    A. Batch system.
    B. Batched, online system.
    C. POS system.
    D. OLRT system.

AICPA.101247BEC

325. During the annual audit, it was learned from an interview with the controller that the accounting system was programmed to use a batch processing method and a detailed posting type. This would mean that individual transactions were

    A. Posted upon entry, and each transaction had its own line entry in the appropriate ledger.
    B. Assigned to groups before posting, and each transaction had its own line entry in the appropriate ledger.
    C. Posted upon entry, and each transaction group had a cumulative entry total in the appropriate ledger.
    D. Assigned to groups before posting, and each transaction group had a cumulative entry total in the appropriate ledger.

Emerging Technologies

Emerging Technologies in AIS

aq.emerg.tech.ais.001_2017

326. The state of emerging online payment systems is:

    A. Increasing reliance on financial institutions.
    B. Improved security.
    C. Improved privacy.
    D. Lower costs to sellers.

aq.emerg.tech.ais.002_2017

327. Alejandro uses Amazon "one-click." This is an example of:

    A. IoT.
    B. Big data.
    C. Smart data.
    D. Payment processing

aq.emerg.tech.ais.003_2017

328. Concerns about the IoT include all of the following **except**:

    A. Reduced privacy.
    B. Cycle times.
    C. Data storage.
    D. Risk exposure.

Emerging Technologies in AIS: Big Data

aq.emerg.tech.ais.001

329. Which of the following is least likely to be an example of big data?

    A. Dark data.
    B. Multifactor identification data.
    C. Sales data.
    D. Video conferencing data.

aq.emerg.tech.ais.002

330. Challenges of big data include all of the following except:

    A. Storage.
    B. Quality.
    C. Integration.
    D. Attrition and retention.

aq.emerg.tech.ais.003

331. Each of the following is an enabler of big data except:

    A. Data warehousing.
    B. Analytics.
    C. Dark data.
    D. IoT.

Bitcoin and Blockchain: Implications for Accounting and Control

aq.bitcoin.001_17

332. The ledger that tracks bitcoins is a(n) _____ ledger while the network that accounts for bitcoins is a(n) _____ network.

    A. Accounting; centralized
    B. Centralized; client-server
    C. Bit furcated; peer-to-peer
    D. Blockchain; peer-to-peer

aq.bitcoin.002_17

333. At Mega-Construction, secured payments are sent to suppliers as soon materials are received and scanned. Many attributes of the received goods are also scanned and recorded immediately on receipt (e.g., time received, quality indicators, item location through GPS functionality). This information is shared through a distributed ledger. Mega-Construction is likely using _____.

    A. Blockchain
    B. TCP/IP
    C. Bitcoin
    D. STMP

aq.bitcoin.003_17

334. Which of the following is an important outcome of the use of blockchain?

    A. Closed-form accounting
    B. Reduced auditing and compliance costs
    C. Increased centralization of accounting systems
    D. Impenetrable authentication

Artificial Intelligence and Machine Learning

aq.ai.learning.001_17

335. Winthrop P. Snigledorf calls about his outrageous cable bill and is greeted by the "voice" of an AI program. This system is probably best described as an example of

    A. Machine learning.
    B. A robot.
    C. An intelligent agent.
    D. An expert system.

aq.ai.learning.002_17

336. AI depends heavily on _____ and _____.

    A. RPA, predictive analytics
    B. Fast computers, big data
    C. Privacy, confidentiality
    D. Analytics, machine learning

aq.ai.learning.003_17

337. Potential short- and medium-term risks of AI include all the following **except**

    A. Machine learning.
    B. Confirmation bias.
    C. Privacy issues.
    D. Prediction bias

Information Security/Availability

Protection of Information

IT Security Principles

aq.it.secur.princ.001_2017

338. _____ concerns whether the system is operational and usable as specified in commitments and agreements.

    A. Security
    B. Availability
    C. Processing integrity
    D. Confidentiality

aq.it.secur.princ.002_2017

339. _____ concerns the completeness, validity, accuracy, timeliness, and authorization of system process.

    A. Quality
    B. Processing integrity
    C. Privacy
    D. Access

aq.it.secur.princ.003_2017

340. _____ is the foundation of systems reliability.

    A. Security
    B. Availability
    C. Processing integrity
    D. Confidentiality

Managing Cyber Risk

aq.mang.cyber.risk.001_2017

341. An item in an organization's newsletter describes a fraud in which cyber criminals pretend to be IT staff who are asking about a system's reliability problem. This is an IT application of the COSO principle of:

    A. The organization obtains or generates and uses relevant, quality information to support the functioning of internal control.

    B. The organization internally communicates information, including objectives and responsibilities for internal control, necessary to support the functioning of internal control.

    C. The organization communicates with external parties regarding matters affecting the functioning of internal control.

    D. The organization selects and develops control activities that contribute to the mitigation of risks to the achievement of objectives to acceptable levels.

aq.mang.cyber.risk.002_2017

342. A consortium of accounting firms shares information about security breaches, including descriptions of cyber attackers and the exploitation methods that they use. This is an IT application of the COSO principle of:

    A. The organization obtains or generates and uses relevant, quality information to support the functioning of internal control.

    B. The organization internally communicates information, including objectives and responsibilities for internal control, necessary to support the functioning of internal control.

    C. The organization communicates with external parties regarding matters affecting the functioning of internal control.

    D. The organization selects and develops control activities that contribute to the mitigation of risks to the achievement of objectives to acceptable levels.

aq.mang.cyber.risk.004_2017

343. In applying COSO to cyber risks, managing cyber risks should begin with:

    A. Informing the board about cyber risks.

    B. Allocating resources to addressing cyberattacks.

    C. Identifying system value.

    D. Cyber risk assessment.

Managing Cyber Risk: Part II—A Framework for Cybersecurity

aq.mang.cyber.risk2.001_17

344. The Slippin' into Darkness Mortuary is reviewing its cybersecurity to explore its current state and related risks as a part of establishing high-level objectives for cybersecurity. In the framework for cybersecurity, this is an example of the element _____ and the function _____.

    A. Categories; identify

    B. Subcategories; respond

    C. References; identify

    D. Functions; detect

aq.mang.cyber.risk2.002_17

345. Which of the following is an inappropriate application of the framework for cybersecurity?

    A. Use the framework to help guide the development and implementation of cybersecurity workforce training related to privacy policies and regulations

    B. Use the framework to help guide the search for referential sources related to a hospital's need to protect patient health care data.

    C. A consortium of small HMOs develops a target cybersecurity profile to guide its members' efforts to create organizationally tailored target profiles.

    D. Replace the organization's existing risk management process with that specified in the framework for cybersecurity.

aq.mang.cyber.risk2.004_17

346. An external auditor is conducting a review of the accounting and control system of Bill's Bad Boy Bagels and Farm Fresh Cream Cheese. Which of the following would be inappropriate in relation to this review?

    A. Use key concepts from the framework for cybersecurity as a basis for explaining the results of the review to Bill's management.

    B. Assure Bill's management that identified deficiencies will be corrected.

    C. Identify the control deficiencies in Bill's system.

    D. Report on the conduct of the engagement to the PCAOB.

IT Policies

aq.it.policies.001_2017

347. Each of the following is a desirable characteristic of IT policies **except**:

    A. Should relate to physical or electronic threats to IT.
    B. An owner is responsible for the policy.
    C. Should include a statement of purpose and a title.
    D. Should be linked to strategy and objectives.

aq.it.policies.002_2017

348. Each of the listed IT policies is matched to its description **except**:

    A. Quality—statement of IT performance standards.
    B. Values and service culture—policies for ensuring the quality of live IT services.
    C. Electronic communications use—policy related to employ use of the Internet, intranet, email, and so on.
    D. Security—related to guarding against physical or electronic threats to IT.

aq.it.policies.003_2017

349. IT policies are particularly important in:

    A. High-tech companies.
    B. Financial services companies.
    C. Decentralized companies.
    D. Companies that sell IT services.

Introduction to E-Business and E-Commerce

aq.it.ebus.001

350. Maxwell's House of Fun asks suppliers to submit proposals to provide its never-ending need for silver hammers. This is an example of:

    A. An e-marketplace.
    B. An electronic exchange.
    C. Viral marketing.
    D. E-procurement.

AICPA.1405045BEC-SIM

351. Which of the following is not a risk of e-commerce?

    A. System availability.
    B. Viral marketing.
    C. Nonrepudiation.
    D. Failure of trust in trading partners.

AICPA.140504BEC-SIM

352. Which of the following is not a risk of e-commerce?

    A. Integrity.
    B. Authentication.
    C. Limited growth.
    D. Security and confidentiality.

E-Commerce Applications

AICPA.060203BEC

353. Which of the following statements is correct concerning the security of messages in an electronic data interchange (EDI) system?

    A. Removable drives that can be locked up at night provide adequate security when the confidentiality of data is the primary risk.
    B. Message authentication in EDI systems performs the same function as segregation of duties in other information systems.
    C. Encryption performed by a physically secure hardware device is more secure than encryption performed by software.
    D. Security at the transaction phase in EDI systems is **not** necessary because problems at that level will be identified by the service provider.

AICPA.061229BEC-SIM

354. Which of the following is not considered to be an electronic funds transfer (EFT) transaction?

    A. Direct deposit of payroll payments into the employee's bank account.
    B. Cash cards.
    C. Automated teller machine (ATM) transactions.
    D. Credit card payment initiated from a POS terminal.

AICPA.101249BEC

355. Which of the following is the primary advantage of using a value-added network (VAN)?

    A. It provides confidentiality for data transmitted over the Internet.
    B. It provides increased security for data transmissions.
    C. It is more cost effective for the company than transmitting data over the Internet.
    D. It enables the company to obtain trend information on data transmissions.

ERM for Cloud Computing

aicpa.aq.erm.cloud.computing.006_17

356. According to COSO, which of the following differences relevant to the risk assessment process is most likely to exist between a large entity and a small entity?

   A. The CEO of a small entity is more likely than the CEO of a large entity to be attuned to risks arising from internal factors through hands-on involvement with all levels of personnel.
   B. The risk assessment process in a small entity is more structured than in a large one because of the nature of some of the internal control components in a small entity.
   C. An owner-manager of a small entity will not normally learn about risks arising from external factors through direct contact with customers, suppliers, and other outsiders, whereas in large entities, this process is part of the entity's primary way of identifying new risk.
   D. Risk assessment in a small entity, as opposed to that in a large entity, can be problematic to implement because the in-depth involvement of the CEO and other key managers is a conflict of interest that must be addressed separately in the internal control assessment process.

aicpa.aq.erm.cloud.computing.007_17

357. A company permits employees to work from home using company-owned laptops. Which of the following competitive advantages does the company most likely obtain as a result of this decision?

   A. Integrity
   B. Reliability
   C. Engagement
   D. Confidentiality

aq.erm.cloud.computing.001_2017

358. Which of the following is most clearly **not** a type of IT outsourcing:

   A. External, public cloud
   B. Internal, public cloud
   C. External, private cloud
   D. Internal, private cloud

Mobile Device, End-User, and Small Business Computing

AICPA.081294BEC-SIM

359. Which of the following statements is true regarding small business computing?

   A. Independent third-party review is especially important.
   B. Backup procedures are important.
   C. Additional supervision of computing may be necessary.
   D. All of the above.

AICPA.130508BEC-SIM

360. Which of the following critical accounting function is most likely to be absent in a small business computing environment?

   A. Authorization.
   B. Record keeping.
   C. Custody.
   D. All of these choices are equally likely to be absent

AICPA.130509BEC-SIM

361. Which of the following strategies is important to managing security over mobile systems?

   A. Hot sites.
   B. BCM.
   C. Teleprinters.
   D. View-only access.

Multi-Location System Structure

aq.it.multi.strctr.001

362. Space Cowboy Amusements operates amusement parks throughout the U.S. Its chief technology officer, Steve Miller, wants to implement a system that allows for more customization to meet the needs of location operations. It most likely will implement:

   A. A centralized system.
   B. Robotics.
   C. A decentralized system.
   D. A hybrid system.

aq.it.multi.strctr.002

363. Cecilia's Breaking My Heart dating service seeks to implement a system that distributes processing to local units but also maintains a centralized database. This is an example of:

   A. A delegated system.
   B. A centralized system.
   C. A decentralized system.
   D. A hybrid system.

AICPA.101062BEC-SIM

364. The multi-location system structure that is sometimes called the "Goldilocks" solution because it seeks to balance design tradeoffs is

    A. Centralized.
    B. Decentralized.
    C. Distributed.
    D. ROM.

Computer Networks and Data Communication

aq.it.ntwrks.001

365. A start-up company seeks to build a wired LAN in its building. Cost is unimportant; security and speed are critical. The company should consider using:

    A. Twisted pair.
    B. Fiber optic cable.
    C. Coaxial cable.
    D. Microwave media.

AICPA.110540BEC-SIM

366. Consider the following statements:

    I.   LANs use dedicated lines.
    II. WANs use dedicated lines.

    A. Both I and II are true.
    B. I is true, but II is not.
    C. II is true, but I is not.
    D. Neither I nor II is true.

AICPA.110541BEC-SIM

367. In walking through O'Hare airport in Chicago, you notice a man talking into an ear piece. The communication between the ear piece and the man's cell phone mostly likely uses which transmission media and protocol?

    A. Fiber optics.
    B. Microwave transmission.
    C. Wi-Fi or spread-spectrum radio transmission.
    D. Bluetooth.

The Internet—Structure and Protocols

AICPA.061214BEC-SIM

368. The data control protocol used to control transmissions on the Internet is

    A. CSMA-CD
    B. TCP/IP
    C. ISP
    D. HTML

AICPA.101259BEC

369. Which of the following technologies is specifically designed to exchange financial information over the World Wide Web?

    A. Hypertext markup language (HTML).
    B. Extensible business reporting language (XBRL).
    C. Hypertext transfer protocol (HTTP).
    D. Transmission control program/Internet protocol (TCP/IP).

IFTC-0052

370. The Internet is made up of a series of networks which include

    A. Gateways to allow mainframe computers to connect to personal computers.
    B. Bridges to direct messages through the optimum data path.
    C. Repeaters to physically connect separate local area networks (LANs).
    D. Routers to strengthen data signals between distant computers.

Logical and Physical Access Controls

Physical Access Controls

AICPA.081283BEC-SIM

371. In an accounting system, a header can be used to

    A. Help format a word processing document.
    B. Identify data records.
    C. Identify file folders.
    D. All of the above.

AICPA.08128BEC-SIM

372. A fire suppression system in a computer facility

    A. Is an application control.
    B. Should include ceiling water outlets.
    C. Should not include halon chemicals.
    D. Is no longer needed in most cases.

IFTC-0025

373. When designing the physical layout of a data processing center, which of the following would be **least** likely to be a necessary control?

    A. Design of controls to restrict access.
    B. Adequate physical layout space for the operating system.
    C. Inclusions of an adequate power supply system with surge protection.
    D. Consideration of risks related to other uses of electricity in the area.

Logical Access Controls

aq.it.logacc.001

374. Eleanor Rigby's Crematorium and Pet Custodian Services wants to choose the strongest control method for accessing its systems. Eleanor should choose:

   A. A sign-in log.
   B. Biometrics.
   C. Passwords.
   D. A two-way mirror.

aq.it.logacc.002

375. Major Tom's Ground Control Flight Services uses biometrics. The control goal of the use of biometrics is:

   A. Accountability.
   B. Authentication.
   C. Authorization.
   D. Certification.

AICPA.061236BEC-SIM

376. Which of the following statements about firewalls is NOT true?

   A. Firewalls frequently include both a hardware component and a software component.
   B. Firewalls screen data packets to determine if they are acceptable or unacceptable and block unacceptable packets from the system.
   C. Application firewalls, in addition to monitoring data packets, control the execution of programs and examine the handling of data by specific applications.
   D. "Network firewall" and "application firewall" are two different names for a program designed to prevent and detect unauthorized access to the system.

Encryption and Secure Exchanges

aq.it.encrpt.001

377. Bob sends a message using asymmetric key to Cassie. In this exchange, who holds the private key:

   A. Bob.
   B. Cassie.
   C. Bob and Cassie.
   D. The server.

AICPA.101260BEC

378. Which of the following solutions creates an encrypted communication tunnel across the Internet for the purpose of allowing a remote user secure access to the network?

   A. Packet-switched network.
   B. Digital encryption.
   C. Authority certificate.
   D. Virtual private network.

IFTC-0017

379. Which of the following would provide the **most** security for sensitive data stored on a personal computer?

   A. Using a secure screen saver program.
   B. Using an eight-bit encoding scheme for hardware interfaces.
   C. Encrypting data files on the computer.
   D. Using a conventional file structure scheme.

System Disruption/Resolution

Organizational Continuity Planning and Disaster Recovery

AICPA.090766.BEC

380. An information technology director collected the names and locations of key vendors, current hardware configuration, names of team members, and an alternative processing location. What is the director most likely preparing?

   A. Data restoration plan.
   B. Disaster recovery plan.
   C. System security policy.
   D. System hardware policy.

AICPA.130511BEC-SIM

381. Which of the following tasks comes first in business continuity management (BCM)?

   A. Embed the BCM in the culture.
   B. Determine business continuity strategies.
   C. Exercise, maintain, and review the plan.
   D. Develop and implement a BCM response

AICPA.130512BEC-SIM

382. In DRP, top priority is given to which activities?

   A. Accounting.
   B. Manufacturing.
   C. Mission critical.
   D. Business critical.

Backup and Restoration

AICPA.081285BEC-SIM

383. A checkpoint is used mostly in _____ systems.

    A. Online real time.
    B. Faulty.
    C. Batch.
    D. General.

AICPA.081287BEC-SIM

384. _____ systems include redundancy of components.

    A. Inefficient.
    B. Online real-time.
    C. Quicken.
    D. Fault tolerant.

AICPA.101248BEC

385. A company has a significant e-commerce presence and self-hosts its website. To assure continuity in the event of a natural disaster, the firm should adopt which of the following strategies?

    A. Back up the server database daily.
    B. Store records off-site.
    C. Purchase and implement RAID technology.
    D. Establish off-site mirrored web server.

Computer Crime, Attack Methods, and Cyber-Incident Response

aq.it.compcrim.001

386. Stagger Lee pretended to be an accountant in the payroll department to gain access to the Wichita Lineman Electrical Services Co. accounting system. This is an example of:

    A. Aliasing.
    B. Malware.
    C. Phishing.
    D. Spoofing.

AICPA.061234BEC-SIM

387. Which of the following is true about denial-of-service attacks?

    I. A denial-of-service attack takes advantage of a network communications protocol to tie up the server's communication ports so that legitimate users cannot gain access to the server.
    II. If the denial-of-service attack is successful, the attacker can gain access to unprotected resources on the server.

    A. I only.
    B. II only.
    C. Both I and II.
    D. Neither I nor II.

AICPA.130715BEC

388. A company's web server has been overwhelmed with a sudden surge of false requests that caused the server to crash. The company has most likely been the target of

    A. Spoofing.
    B. Piggybacking.
    C. An eavesdropping attack.
    D. A denial of service attack.

Processing Integrity (Input/Processing/Output Controls)

Program Library, Documentation, and Record Management

aicpa.aq.it.appctrl.lib.doc.001_17

389. The most appropriate data-gathering techniques for a system survey include interviews, quick questionnaires, observations, and

    A. Prototypes.
    B. Systems documentation.
    C. PERT charts.
    D. Gantt charts.

AICPA.101039BEC-SIM

390. After changes to a source program have been made and verified, it moves to

    A. Atlanta.
    B. Development.
    C. The operator.
    D. Production.

AICPA.120617BEC

391. Management of a company has a lack of segregation of duties within the application environment, with programmers having access to development and production. The programmers have the ability to implement application code changes into production without monitoring or a quality assurance function. This is considered a deficiency in which of the following areas?

    A. Change control.
    B. Management override.
    C. Data integrity.
    D. Computer operations.

Input and Origination Controls

aicpa.aq.it.appctrl.inpt.001_17

392. A customer notified a company that the customer's account did not reflect the most recent monthly payment. The company investigated the issue and determined that a clerk had mistakenly applied the customer's payments to a different customer's account. Which of the following controls would help to prevent such an error?

    A. Checksum
    B. Field check
    C. Completeness test
    D. Closed-loop verification

AICPA.090772.BEC

393. An employee mistakenly enters April 31 in the date field. Which of the following programmed edit checks offers the best solution for detecting this error?

    A. Online prompting.
    B. Mathematical accuracy.
    C. Preformatted screen.
    D. Reasonableness.

AICPA.130721BEC

394. An entity has the following sales orders in a batch:

Invoice#	Product	Quantity	Unit Price
101	K 10	50	$ 5.00
102	M 15	100	$10.00
103	P 20	150	$25.00
104	Q 25	200	$30.00
105	T 30	250	$35.00

Which of the following numbers represents the record count?

    A. 5
    B. 100
    C. 105
    D. 750

Processing, File, and Output Controls

AICPA.040220BEC-SIM

395. A poor quality connection caused extensive line noise, resulting in faulty data transmission. Which of the following controls is most likely to detect this condition?

    A. Line check.
    B. Batch control total.
    C. Closed loop verification.
    D. Parity check.

AICPA.060628BEC

396. An auditor was examining a client's network and discovered that the users did not have any password protection.

    Which of the following would be the best example of the type of network password the users should have?

    A. trjunpqs.
    B. 34787761.
    C. tr34ju78.
    D. tR34ju78.

AICPA.101035BEC-SIM

397. The distribution of reports is considered what type of control?

    A. Input.
    B. Processing.
    C. Output.
    D. Software.

Accounting System Cycles

The Accounting System Cycle: Introduction

aq.acct.sys.cyc.intro.001

398. The accounting cycle begins by recording _____ in the form of journal entries.

    A. Business transactions.
    B. Financial information.
    C. Corporate minutes.
    D. Business contracts.

aq.acct.sys.cyc.intro.002

399. After journal entries are recorded, they are posted to:

    A. General journals.
    B. Ledger accounts.
    C. Income statement.
    D. Expense reports.

aq.acct.sys.cyc.intro.003_17

400. The financing cycle contributes _____ to the expenditure cycle, which contributes _____ to the production cycle.

    A. Revenue, expenditures
    B. Raw materials, finished products
    C. Labor, raw materials
    D. Funds, raw materials

Revenue Cycle

aq.rev.cyc.001

401. The most important document in the billing process is the

    A. Picking ticket.
    B. Sales invoice.
    C. Packing slip.
    D. Bill of lading.

aq.rev.cyc.002

402. Hildegard works at Amazon in the warehouse. What is the screen called that she most likely uses to assemble the goods for customers' orders for shipping?

    A. Sales order.
    B. Invoice.
    C. Picking ticket.
    D. Bill of lading.

aq.rev.cyc.003

403. Harold is a sales person at a jeweler. His friend Robert wants to buy a ring for his fiancée. Who should establish the credit limit for Robert's purchase?

    A. Harold.
    B. The credit manager.
    C. The sales manager.
    D. Any of the above.

Expenditure Cycle

aq.expend.cyc.001

404. Reggie is the purchasing agent for a wholesale paint store (Ye Ol' Paint Pots). Reggie's cousin, Earl-the-Earl, owns a small paint store. Reggie arranged for paint to be delivered to Earl-the-Earl's stores from paint manufacturers, thereby allowing Earl-the-Earl to get the paint at a wholesale (cheaper) price, which violates a policy of the Ye Ol' Paint Pots. Reggie was most likely able to violate this policy because of a failure in Ye Ol' Paint Pots' controls related to:

    A. Purchase orders.
    B. Cash disbursements.
    C. Bills of lading.
    D. Inventory control.

aq.expend.cyc.002_2017

405. Reggie is the purchasing agent for a wholesale paint store (Ye Ol' Paint Pots) that sells only to large chains. Reggie's cousin, Earl the Earl, owns a small paint store. Reggie arranged for paint to be delivered from paint manufacturers to Earl the Earl's store, thereby allowing Earl the Earl to get the paint at a wholesale (cheaper) price, which violates a policy of Ye Ol' Paint Pots. The control that is most likely to have prevented this violation of policy is:

    A. Segregation of the receiving function from the purchasing function
    B. Monitoring whether discounts are taken in purchasing
    C. Requiring purchasing agents to disclose relationships with vendors and purchases
    D. Automated receiving

aq.expend.cyc.003

406. Happy's Nutty Clownery ordered 82 bags of balloons from a supplier but received only 28. Which of the following controls is most likely to have caught this error?

    A. Separation of duties in cash receipts
    B. Formalizing the process for authorizing the purchase of goods
    C. Requiring purchasing agents to disclose relationships with vendors and purchasers
    D. An automated receiving system that includes multiple points of scanning of received goods

Production Cycle

aq.prod.cyc.001

407. Hamish works in a factory that builds tractors in Des Moines, Iowa. He wants to get a B352 sprocket that is needed in building a X793 tractor. The document, form, or screen that would authorize this action is:

    A. Bill of materials.
    B. Materials requisition.
    C. Move ticket.
    D. Picking ticket.

aq.prod.cyc.002

408. Hamish works in a factory that builds tractors in Des Moines, Iowa. He can't remember whether the B352 or the C917 sprocket is needed in building a X793 tractor. The document, form, or screen that would help him decide is:

    A. Bill of materials.
    B. Materials requisition.
    C. Move ticket.
    D. Picking ticket.

aq.prod.cyc.003_17

409. A master production schedule is **most** likely to be useful in

    A. Identifying erroneous journal entries.
    B. Inventory shrinkage.
    C. Pricing of goods for sale.
    D. Reducing excess production of inventory.

HR and Payroll Cycle

aq.hr.pay.cyc.001

410. Requiring direct deposits instead of paying employees by checks improves accounting controls by:

    A. Separating duties in cash receipts.
    B. Reducing the likelihood of the theft of payroll payments.
    C. Facilitating advanced analytics of payroll data.
    D. Reducing the risk of violations of employment law.

aq.hr.pay.cyc.002

411. What document is useful in determining which employee should be assigned a new job duty?

    A. U.S. form 941.
    B. Workforce inventory.
    C. Skills inventory report.
    D. Cumulative earnings register.

aq.hr.pay.cyc.003

412. James Victor's Snickers Joke House hires illegal workers. Which of the core activities of the HR department should have identified and prevented this violation of law?

    A. Complying with laws and regulations.
    B. Training and development.
    C. Salaries and benefits.
    D. Recruiting and hiring employees.

General Ledger, Reporting, and Financing Cycle

aq.gen.led.rep.cyc.001

413. Reconciling the accounts receivable control and subsidiary accounts is useful in ensuring that:

    A. All recorded balances are active.
    B. All credit sales transactions are recorded.
    C. Stockouts are unlikely.
    D. Prenumbered shipping documents match sales.

aq.gen.led.rep.cyc.002

414. In the accounting cycle, closing journal entries:

    A. Identify and record all liabilities, revenues, and expenses at the end of the fiscal year.
    B. Ensure the matching of revenue and expenses by period.
    C. Transfer balances in temporary accounts to retained earnings.
    D. Lessen the likelihood of deceptive manual journal entries.

aq.gen.led.rep.cyc.003_17

415. Adjusting journal entries are of additional concern when they are

    A. Automated accruals or deferrals,
    B. RFID driven,
    C. Unusual and automated.
    D. Unusual and manually posted.

Systems Development and Maintenance

System Development and Implementation

aicpa.aq.it.syst.dev.imp.003_17

416. At what phase in the systems development process is a report generated that describes the content, processing flows, resource requirements, and procedures of a preliminary system design?

    A. File and database design
    B. Conceptual systems design
    C. Physical systems design
    D. Procedures design

aq.sys.dev.main.002

417. Mr. Shankley's Medical Services Corp. operates in all states and territories of the U.S. It is developing a new patient relationship management system. The system is approaching completion and is behind schedule. Which of the following implementation methods would be potentially fastest but also involve the most risk?

    A. Pilot testing.
    B. Direct cutover.
    C. Phased implementation.
    D. Parallel implementation.

AICPA.08011647BEC.IV

418. Which of the following implementation approaches has been described as "sink or swim?"

    A. Parallel.
    B. Cold turkey.
    C. Phased.
    D. Pilot.

Operations Management

Financial and Nonfinancial Measures of Performance

Quality Management

AICPA.940545BEC-AR

419. In a quality control program, which of the following is (are) categorized as internal failure costs?

    I. Rework.
    II. Responding to customer complaints.
    III. Statistical quality control procedures.

    A. I only.
    B. II only.
    C. III only.
    D. I, II, and III.

AICPA.940550BEC-AR

420. Bell Co. changed from a traditional manufacturing philosophy to a just-in-time philosophy.

    What are the expected effects of this change on Bell's inventory turnover and inventory as a percentage of total assets reported on Bell's balance sheet?

	Inventory turnover	Inventory percentage
A.	Decrease	Decrease
B.	Decrease	Increase
C.	Increase	Decrease
D.	Increase	Increase

assess.AICPA.BEC.qual.int.mgmt-0033

421. Which of the following methodologies would be most effective for a company that wants to reduce its rate of defective products?

    A. Break-even analysis.
    B. Six Sigma.
    C. Variable costing.
    D. Sensitivity analysis.

Balanced Scorecard and Benchmarking

AICPA.060624BEC

422. Which of the following balanced scorecard perspectives examines a company's success in targeted market segments?

    A. Financial.
    B. Customer.
    C. Internal business process.
    D. Learning and growth.

AICPA.090626BEC-V-B

423. The management of a company would do which of the following to compare and contrast its financial information to published information reflecting optimal amounts?

    A. Budget.
    B. Forecast.
    C. Benchmark.
    D. Utilize best practices.

AICPA.950546BEC-AR

424. Which measures would be useful in evaluating the performance of a manufacturing system?

    I. Throughput time.
    II. Total setup time for machines/Total production time.
    III. Number of rework units/Total number of units completed.

    A. I and II only.
    B. II and III only.
    C. I and III only.
    D. I, II, and III.

assess.AICPA.BEC.bal.sccrd-0032

425. Which of the following types of performance measures integrates financial performance, internal operations, learning and growth, and customer satisfaction?

    A. Total productivity
    B. Financial ratio analysis
    C. Balanced scorecard
    D. Benchmarking

Competitive Analysis

AICPA.101160BEC

426. Wexford Co. has a subunit that reported the following data for year 1:

Asset (investment) turnover	1.5 times
Sales	$750,000
Return on sales	8%

The imputed interest rate is 12%. What is the division residual income for year 1?

- A. $60,000.
- B. $30,000.
- C. $20,000.
- D. $0.

AICPA.101161BEC

427. The target capital structure of Traggle Co. is 50% debt, 10% preferred equity, and 40% common equity. The interest rate on debt is 6%, the yield on the preferred is 7%, the cost of common equity is 11.5%, and the tax rate is 40%. Traggle does not anticipate issuing any new stock. What is Traggle's weighted average cost of capital?

- A. 6.50%.
- B. 6.77%.
- C. 7.10%.
- D. 8.30%.

assess.AICPA.BEC.comptv.anls-0028

428. A company is trying to determine the cost of capital for a major expansion project. A survey of commercial lenders indicates that cost of debt is currently 8% based on the company's debt ratio of 40%. The company complies with this requirement and has determined that a stock issuance would require a 10% return in order to attract investors. Which of the following is the company's cost of capital?

- A. 8.8%
- B. 9.2%
- C. 10.6%
- D. 18.0%

Ratio Analysis

assess.AICPA.BEC.rtio.anls-0027

429. Management would like to calculate return on investment (ROI) for the current year. The following information is available:

Operating assets at the end of the year	$ 6,600,000
Operating assets at the beginning of the year	5,400,000
Sales	1,150,000
Operating expenses	550,000

What percentage amount is the ROI?

- A. 9%
- B. 10%
- C. 11%
- D. 19%

AICPA.090620BEC-V-B

430. To measure inventory management performance, a company monitors its inventory turnover ratio. Listed below are selected data from the company's accounting records:

	Current year	Prior year
Annual sales	$2,525,000	$2,125,000
Gross profit percent	40%	35%

Beginning finished goods inventory for the current year was 15% of the prior year's annual sales, and ending finished goods inventory was 22% of the current year's annual sales. What was the company's inventory turnover at the end of the current period?

- A. 1.82.
- B. 2.31.
- C. 2.73.
- D. 3.47.

AICPA.101162BEC

431. Galax, Inc. had an operating income of $5,000,000 before interest and taxes. Galax's net book value of plant assets on January 1 and December 31 were $22,000,000 and $18,000,000, respectively. Galax achieved a 25% return on investment for the year, with an investment turnover of 2.5. What were Galax's sales for the year?

- A. $55,000,000.
- B. $50,000,000.
- C. $45,000,000.
- D. $20,000,000.

Risk Management

AICPA.100965BEC-V-SIM

432. Why is cost avoidance a faster way to increase profits than to increase revenue?

    A. Cost avoidance is part of a well thought out strategic approach.
    B. Increasing revenue often results in at least some proportional cost increases.
    C. Cost avoidance targets committed costs.
    D. Efforts to increase revenue relate to committed costs only.

AICPA.100966BEC-V-SIM

433. Which of the following types of risk are best addressed with insurance?

    A. Peril or hazard.
    B. Speculative risks.
    C. Price risk.
    D. Portfolio risk.

AICPA.100967BEC-V-SIM

434. Which of the following types of risk are best addressed with hedging?

    A. Strategic and operating risk.
    B. Foreign currency exchange.
    C. Disaster recovery.
    D. Liquidity.

AICPA.100968BEC-V-SIM

435. Which of the following terms describe or are consistent with systematic risk?

    A. Portfolio risk.
    B. Market risk.
    C. Diversifiable risk.
    D. Company-specific risk.

Performance Improvement Tools

AICPA.101063BEC-SIM

436. Which of the following production processes best describes lean manufacturing?

    A. Making a small number of a high variety of unique products with relatively low-skilled labor.
    B. Making a large number of standardized products with highly skilled labor.
    C. Making small batches of a high variety of unique products with cross-trained labor.
    D. Making a large number of standardized products with relatively low-skilled labor.

AICPA.101065BEC-SIM

437. What is the objective of the demand flow approach?

    A. To link process flows and manage them based on customer demand.
    B. To mathematically link "push-based" inventory features.
    C. To mathematically facilitate constraint management.
    D. To mathematically assist disruptive flow management in forecasting.

AICPA.101066BEC-SIM

438. What tools does Six Sigma commonly use to achieve quality control?

    A. Demand flow technology tools (e.g., continuous flow planning).
    B. Tools common to TQM (e.g., control charts).
    C. Constraint management optimization tools (e.g., capacity analysis).
    D. Push-model tools (e.g., forecasting using regression).

Cost Accounting

Manufacturing Costs

AICPA.130731BEC

439. A company is considering outsourcing one of the component parts for its product. The company currently makes 10,000 parts per month. Current costs are as follows:

	Per unit	Total
Direct materials	$4	$40,000
Direct labor	3	30,000
Fixed plant facility cost	2	20,000

The company decides to purchase the part for $8 per unit from another supplier and rents its idle capacity for $5,000/month. How will the company's monthly costs change?

    A. Decrease $15,000.
    B. Decrease $10,000.
    C. Increase $5,000.
    D. Increase $10,000.

AICPA.920551BEC-TH-AR

440. In a process cost system, the application of factory overhead usually would be recorded as an increase in

    A. Finished goods inventory control.
    B. Factory overhead control.
    C. Cost of goods sold.
    D. Work-in-process inventory control.

AICPA.930541BEC-TH-AR

441. In a traditional job order cost system, the issue of indirect materials to a production department increases

    A. Stores control.
    B. Work in process control.
    C. Factory overhead control.
    D. Factory overhead applied.

Spoilage, Cost, and Inventory Flow

AICPA.911144BEC-TH-AR

442. In June, Delta Co. experienced scrap, normal spoilage, and abnormal spoilage in its manufacturing process. The cost of units produced includes

    A. Scrap, but not spoilage.
    B. Normal spoilage, but neither scrap nor abnormal spoilage.
    C. Scrap and normal spoilage, but not abnormal spoilage.
    D. Scrap, normal spoilage, and abnormal spoilage.

AICPA.920548BEC-P2-AR

443. Hoyt Co. manufactured the following units:

Saleable	5,000
Unsaleable (normal spoilage)	200
Unsaleable (abnormal spoilage)	300

The manufacturing cost totaled $99,000. What amount should Hoyt debit to finished goods?

    A. $90,000.
    B. $93,600.
    C. $95,400.
    D. $99,000.

AICPA.950541BEC-AR

444. In its April Year 1 production, Hern Corp., which does not use a standard cost system, incurred total production costs of $900,000, of which Hern attributed $60,000 to normal spoilage and $30,000 to abnormal spoilage.

Hern should account for this spoilage as

    A. Period cost of $90,000.
    B. Inventoriable cost of $90,000.
    C. Period cost of $60,000 and inventoriable cost of $30,000.
    D. Inventoriable cost of $60,000 and period cost of $30,000.

assess.AICPA.BEC.spl.invent-0002

445. A company estimates that it will sell 100,000 units of finished goods in March. Each finished good requires 5 feet of raw materials. The projected March 1 inventory balances are 10,000 units of finished goods and 40,000 feet of raw materials. Desired March 31 inventory levels are 9,000 units of finished goods and 42,000 feet of raw materials. What amount of raw materials should the company plan to purchase during March?

    A. 497,000 feet.
    B. 500,000 feet.
    C. 502,000 feet.
    D. 503,000 feet.

Cost Behavior Patterns

AICPA.101168BEC

446. A delivery company is implementing a system to compare the costs of purchasing and operating different vehicles in its fleet. Truck 415 is driven 125,000 miles per year at a variable cost of $0.13 per mile. Truck 415 has a capacity of 28,000 pounds and delivers 250 full loads per year. What amount is the truck's delivery cost per pound?

    A. $0.00163 per pound.
    B. $0.00232 per pound.
    C. $0.58036 per pound.
    D. $1.72000 per pound.

AICPA.951139BEC-AR

447. Sender, Inc. estimates parcel mailing costs using the data shown on the chart below.

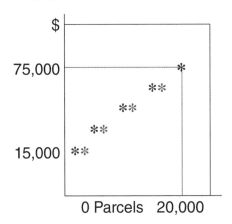

What is Sender's estimated cost for mailing 12,000 parcels?

    A. $36,000.
    B. $45,000.
    C. $51,000.
    D. $60,000.

Cost-Volume-Profit Analysis

AICPA.120602BEC

448. A ceramics manufacturer sold cups last year for $7.50 each. Variable costs of manufacturing were $2.25 per unit. The company needed to sell 20,000 cups to break even. Net income was $5,040. This year, the company expects the following changes: sales price per cup to be $9.00; variable manufacturing costs to increase 33.3%; fixed costs to increase 10%; and the income tax rate to remain at 40%. Sales in the coming year are expected to exceed last year's sales by 1,000 units. How many units does the company expect to sell this year?

   A. 21,000
   B. 21,600
   C. 21,960
   D. 22,600

AICPA.120610BEC

449. State College is using cost-volume-profit analysis to determine tuition rates for the upcoming school year. Projected costs for the year are as follows:

Contribution margin per student	$ 1,800
Variable expenses per student	1,000
Total fixed expenses	360,000

Based on these estimates, what is the approximate break-even point in number of students?

   A. 129
   B. 200
   C. 360
   D. 450

AICPA.130737BEC

450. Trendy Co. produced and sold 30,000 backpacks during the last year at an average price of $25 per unit. Unit variable costs were the following:

Variable manufacturing costs	$9
Variable selling and administrative costs	6
Total	$15

Total fixed costs were $250,000. There was no year-end work-in-process inventory. If Trendy had spent an additional $15,000 on advertising, then sales would have increased by $30,000. If Trendy had made this investment, what change would have occurred in Trendy's pretax profit?

   A. $3,000 increase.
   B. $4,200 increase.
   C. $3,000 decrease.
   D. $4,200 decrease.

Absorption and Direct Costing

AICPA.920549BEC-P2-AR

451. At the end of Killo Co.'s first year of operations, 1,000 units of inventory remained on hand. Variable and fixed manufacturing costs per unit were $90 and $20, respectively. If Killo uses absorption costing rather than direct (variable) costing, the result would be a higher pretax income of

   A. $0.
   B. $20,000.
   C. $70,000.
   D. $90,000.

AICPA.930545BEC-TH-AR

452. A manufacturing company prepares income statements using both absorption and variable costing methods. At the end of a period, actual sales revenues, total gross profit, and total contribution margin approximated budgeted figures, whereas income was substantially greater than the budgeted amount. There were no beginning or ending inventories.

The most likely explanation of the income increase is that, compared to budget, actual

   A. Manufacturing fixed costs had increased.
   B. Selling and administrative fixed expenses had decreased.
   C. Sales prices and variable costs had increased proportionately.
   D. Sales prices had declined proportionately less than variable costs.

AICPA.951156BEC-AR

453. Lynn Manufacturing Co. prepares income statements using both standard absorption and standard variable costing methods. For Year 2, unit standard costs were unchanged from Year 1. In Year 2, the only beginning and ending inventories were finished goods of 5,000 units.

How would Lynn's ratios using absorption costing compare with those using variable costing?

	Current Ratio	Return on Stockholders' Equity
A.	Same	Same
B.	Same	Smaller
C.	Greater	Same
D.	Greater	Smaller

Job Costing

AICPA.130731BEC

454. A company is considering outsourcing one of the component parts for its product. The company currently makes 10,000 parts per month. Current costs are as follows:

	Per unit	Total
Direct materials	$4	$40,000
Direct labor	3	30,000
Fixed plant facility cost	2	20,000

The company decides to purchase the part for $8 per unit from another supplier and rents its idle capacity for $5,000/month. How will the company's monthly costs change?

A. Decrease $15,000.
B. Decrease $10,000.
C. Increase $5,000.
D. Increase $10,000.

AICPA.911143BEC-TH-AR

455. A direct labor overtime premium should be charged to a specific job when the overtime is caused by the

A. Increased overall level of activity.
B. Customer's requirement for the early completion of a job.
C. Management's failure to include the job in the production schedule.
D. Management's requirement that the job be completed before the annual factory vacation closure.

AICPA.920544BEC-P2-AR

456. Birk Co. uses a job order cost system. The following debits (credits) appeared in Birk's work in process account for the month of April Year 1:

April	Description	Amount
1	Balance	$4,000
30	Direct materials	24,000
30	Direct labor	16,000
30	Factory overhead	12,800
30	To finished goods	(48,000)

Birk applies overhead to production at a predetermined rate of 80% of the direct labor cost. Job No. 5, the only job still in process on April 30, Year 1, was charged with direct labor of $2,000. What was the amount of direct materials charged to Job No. 5?

A. $3,000.
B. $5,200.
C. $8,800.
D. $24,000.

Process Costing

AICPA.060223BEC-TH-AR

457. Black, Inc. employs a weighted average method in its process costing system. Black's work in process inventory on June 30 consists of 40,000 units. These units are 100% complete with respect to materials and 60% complete with respect to conversion costs. The equivalent unit costs are $5.00 for materials and $7.00 for conversion costs.

What is the total cost of the June 30 work in process inventory?

A. $200,000.
B. $288,000.
C. $368,000.
D. $480,000.

AICPA.060618BEC

458. During the current year, the following manufacturing activity took place for a company's products:

- Beginning work in process: 10,000 units, 70% complete
- Units started into production during the year: 150,000 units
- Units completed during the year: 140,000 units
- Ending work in process: 20,000 units, 25% complete
- What was the number of equivalent units produced using the first-in, first-out method?

A. 138,000.
B. 140,000.
C. 145,000.
D. 150,000.

AICPA.900542BEC-TH-AR

459. In process 2, material G is added when a batch is 60% complete. Ending work in process units, which are 50% complete, would be included in the computation of equivalent units for

	Conversion costs	Material G
A.	Yes	No
B.	No	Yes
C.	No	No
D.	Yes	Yes

Joint and By-Product Costing

AICPA.090624BEC-V-C

460. Which of the following is not a basic approach to allocating costs for costing inventory in joint-cost situations?

A. Sales value at split-off.
B. Flexible budget amounts.
C. Physical measures, such as weights or volume.
D. Constant gross margin percentage net realizable value method.

AICPA.130728BEC

461. LM Enterprises produces two products in a common production process, each of which is processed further after the split-off point. Joint costs incurred for the current month are $36,000. The following information for the current month was

Product	Units Produced	Units Sold	Separable Costs	Selling Price Per Unit
L	10,000	9,500	$20,000	$ 8
M	5,000	4,000	40,000	20

What amount would be the joint cost allocated to product M, assuming that LM Enterprises uses the estimated net realizable value method to allocate costs?

A. $20,000
B. $12,000
C. $15,000
D. $18,000

AICPA.950543BEC-AR

462. Kode Co. manufactures a major product that gives rise to a by-product called May. May's only separable cost is a $1 selling cost when a unit is sold for $4. Kode accounts for May's sales by deducting the $3 net amount from the cost of goods sold of the major product. There are no inventories.

If Kode were to change its method of accounting for May from a by-product to a joint product, what would be the effect on Kode's overall gross margin?

A. No effect.
B. Gross margin increases by $1 for each unit of May sold.
C. Gross margin increases by $3 for each unit of May sold.
D. Gross margin increases by $4 for each unit of May sold.

Sales and Direct Cost Variance Analysis

AICPA.120608BEC

463. For the current period production levels, XL Molding Co. budgeted 8,500 board feet of production and used 9,000 board feet for actual production. Material cost was budgeted at $2 per foot. The actual cost for the period was $3 per foot. What was XL's material efficiency variance for the period?

A. $1,000 favorable.
B. $1,000 unfavorable.
C. $1,500 favorable.
D. $1,500 unfavorable.

AICPA.130735BEC

464. Selected costs associated with a product are as follows:

Total standard hours for units produced	5,000
Total actual direct labor cost	$111,625.00
Actual per hour labor rate	$23.50
Standard per hour labor rate	$24.00

What amount is the total direct labor price variance?

A. $2,375 unfavorable.
B. $2,375 favorable.
C. $2,500 unfavorable.
D. $2,500 favorable.

assess.AICPA.BEC.dir.cst.var.anls-0030

465. A company produces widgets with budgeted standard direct materials of 2 pounds per widget at $5 per pound. Standard direct labor was budgeted at 0.5 hour per widget at $15 per hour. The actual usage in the current year was 25,000 pounds and 3,000 hours to produce 10,000 widgets. What was the direct material usage variance?

A. $25,000 favorable.
B. $25,000 unfavorable.
C. $30,000 favorable.
D. $30,000 unfavorable.

Overhead Variance Analysis

AICPA.910543BEC-TH-AR

466. In Year 1, a department's three-variance overhead standard costing system reported unfavorable spending and volume variances. The activity level selected for allocating overhead to the product was based on 80% of practical capacity.

If 100% of practical capacity had been selected instead, how would the reported unfavorable spending and volume variances have been affected?

	Spending variance	Volume variance
A.	Increased	Unchanged
B.	Increased	Increased
C.	Unchanged	Increased
D.	Unchanged	Unchanged

AICPA.921125BEC-P2-AR

467. The following information pertains to Roe Co.'s Year 1 manufacturing operations:

Standard direct labor hours per unit	2
Actual direct labor hours	10,500
Number of units produced	5,000
Standard variable overhead per standard direct labor hour	$3
Actual variable overhead	$28,000

Roe's Year 1 unfavorable variable overhead efficiency variance was

A. $0.
B. $1,500.
C. $2,000.
D. $3,500.

AICPA.930543BEC-TH-AR

468. Which of the following standard costing variances would be least controllable by a production supervisor?

A. Overhead volume.
B. Overhead efficiency.
C. Labor efficiency.
D. Material usage.

Process Management

Cost Relevance

AICPA.040151BEC-SIM

469. Which one of the following costs, if any, is relevant when making financial decisions?

	Sunk Costs	Opportunity Costs
A.	Yes	Yes
B.	Yes	No
C.	No	Yes
D.	No	No

AICPA.08211311BEC.V.E

470. Which of the following items is never relevant to a sell or process further decision?

A. Incremental revenue after the split-off point.
B. Incremental cost after the split-off point.
C. Joint costs.
D. Additional contribution margin realized if processed further.

Special Decisions

AICPA.060614BEC

471. Rodder, Inc. manufactures a component in a router assembly. The selling price and unit cost data for the component are as follows:

Selling price	$15
Direct materials cost	3
Direct labor cost	3
Variable overhead cost	3
Fixed manufacturing overhead cost	2
Fixed selling and administration cost	1

The company received a special one-time order for 1,000 components. Rodder has an alternative use for production capacity for the 1,000 components that would produce a contribution margin of $5,000. What amount is the lowest unit price Rodder should accept for the component?

A. $9.
B. $12.
C. $14.
D. $24.

AICPA.08211329BEC.V.E

472. A company receives an offer to purchase a special order of units of a product that normally sells for $10 each to regular customers. The cost of manufacturing the units is shown here. If all other conditions are favorable, what is the absolute lowest price that the company would be able to feasibly accept for the order if it has enough idle capacity to handle the order?

	Cost per unit
Direct materials	$2
Direct labor	$1
Avoidable fixed costs	$2
Unavoidable fixed costs	$3

A. $5.
B. $8.
C. $3.
D. $10.

AICPA.08211330BEC.V.E

473. Tennis rackets can be purchased for $60 each from an outside vendor. It costs the manufacturer $80 a piece to produce them, of which 30% is unavoidable fixed overhead cost. What are the relevant costs for this decision? Based only on these costs, which option should the company choose?

	Relevant Costs	Buy and Make Decision
A.	$60 and $56	Make
B.	$60 and $56	Buy
C.	$56 and $24	Buy
D.	$56 and $24	Make

AICPA.940549BEC-AR

474. Clay Co. has considerable excess manufacturing capacity. A special job order's cost sheet includes the following applied manufacturing overhead costs:

Fixed costs	$21,000
Variable costs	33,000

The fixed costs include a normal $3,700 allocation for in-house design costs, although no in-house design will be done. Instead the job will require the use of external designers costing $7,750.

What is the total amount to be included in the calculation to determine the minimum acceptable price for the job?

A. $36,700.
B. $40,750.
C. $54,000.
D. $58,050.

assess.AICPA.BEC.rel.csts.2-0029

475. The following information is available on Tackler Co.'s two product lines:

	Chairs	Tables
Sales	$180,000	$48,000
Variable costs	(96,000)	(30,000)
Contribution margin	84,000	18,000
Fixed costs:		
Avoidable	(36,000)	(12,000)
Unavoidable	(18,000)	(10,800)
Operating income (loss)	$ 30,000	($ 4,800)

Assuming Tackler discontinues the tables line and does not replace it, the company's operating income will

A. Increase by $4,800.
B. Increase by $6,000.
C. Decrease by $6,000.
D. Decrease by $10,800.

Transfer Pricing

AICPA.082113116BEC.V.A

476. In the GPK Coffee Company, the Strudel Division has strudel that can be sold either to outside customers or to the Bean Division that also sells coffee. Information about these divisions is given below:

	Case 1	Case 2
Strudel Division:		
Capacity in units of strudel	1,000	1,000
Number of units sold or demanded externally	600	1,000
Market selling price	$2.00	$1.50
Avoidable outlay costs per unit	$1.50	$1.30
Unavoidable costs per unit based on capacity	$0.20	$0.20
Bean Division:		
Number of units of strudel needed	400	400
Budgeted price per unit	$1.95	$1.45

Given the facts in case 2, what are the minimum and maximum transfer prices?

	Minimum	Maximum
A.	$1.45	$1.50
B.	$1.50	$2.00
C.	$1.30	$1.50
D.	$1.50	$1.50

AICPA.08211315BEC.V.A

477. In the GPK Coffee Company, the Strudel Division has strudel that can be sold either to outside customers or to the Bean Division that also sells coffee. Information about these divisions is given below:

	Case 1	Case 2
Strudel Division:		
Capacity in units of strudel	1,000	1,000
Number of units sold or demanded externally	600	1,000
Market selling price	$2.00	$1.50
Avoidable outlay costs per unit	$1.50	$1.30
Unavoidable costs per unit based on capacity	$0.20	$0.20
Bean Division:		
Number of units of strudel needed	400	400
Budgeted price per unit	$1.95	$1.45

Given the facts in case 1, what are the minimum and maximum transfer prices?

	Minimum	Maximum
A.	$1.95	$2.00
B.	$1.50	$2.00
C.	$1.30	$1.95
D.	$1.50	$1.95

AICPA.08211317BEC.V.A

478. In the GPK Coffee Company, the Strudel Division has strudel that can be sold either to outside customers or to the Bean Division that also sells coffee. Information about these divisions is given below:

	Case 1	Case 2
Strudel Division:		
Capacity in units of strudel	1,000	1,000
Number of units sold or demanded externally	600	1,000
Market selling price	$2.00	$1.50
Avoidable outlay costs per unit	$1.50	$1.30
Unavoidable costs per unit based on capacity	$0.20	$0.20
Bean Division:		
Number of units of strudel needed	400	400
Budgeted price per unit	$1.95	$1.45

Will the internal transfer likely take place? Answer for Case 1 and 2 separately.

	Case 1	Case 2
A.	Yes	Yes
B.	Yes	No
C.	No	Yes
D.	No	No

AICPA.940544BEC-AR

479. Brent Co. has intracompany service transfers from Division Core, a cost center, to Division Pro, a profit center. Under stable economic conditions, which of the following transfer prices is likely to be most conducive to evaluating whether both divisions have met their responsibilities?

A. Actual cost.
B. Standard variable cost.
C. Actual cost plus mark-up.
D. Negotiated price.

Activity-Based Costing and Process Management

AICPA.130729BEC

480. A manufacturing company has several product lines. Traditionally, it has allocated manufacturing overhead costs between product lines based on total machine hours for each product line. Under a new activity-based costing system, which of the following overhead costs would be most likely to have a new cost driver assigned to it?

A. Electricity expense.
B. Repair and maintenance expense.
C. Employee benefits expense.
D. Depreciation expense.

AICPA.920555BEC-TH-AR

481. Book Co. uses the activity-based costing approach for cost allocation and product costing purposes. Printing, cutting, and binding functions make up the manufacturing process. Machinery and equipment are arranged in operating cells that produce a complete product starting with raw materials.

Which of the following are characteristic of Book's activity-based costing approach?

I. Cost drivers are used as a basis for cost allocation.
II. Costs are accumulated by department or function for the purposes of product costing.
III. Activities that do not add value to the product are identified and reduced to the extent possible.

A. I only.
B. I and II.
C. I and III.
D. II and III.

AICPA.921145BEC-TH-AR

482. Nile Co.'s cost allocation and product costing procedures follow activity-based costing principles. Activities have been identified and classified as being either value-adding or nonvalue-adding as to each product.

Which of the following activities, used in Nile's production process, is nonvalue-adding?

A. Design engineering activity.
B. Heat treatment activity.
C. Drill press activity.
D. Raw materials storage activity.

AICPA.931145BEC-TH-AR

483. In an activity-based costing system, cost reduction is accomplished by identifying and eliminating

	All Cost Drivers	Nonvalue-Adding Activities
A.	No	No
B.	Yes	Yes
C.	No	Yes
D.	Yes	No

AICPA.940541BEC-AR

484. What is the normal effect on the numbers of cost pools and allocation bases when an activity-based cost (ABC) system replaces a traditional cost system?

	Cost Pools	Allocation Bases
A.	No effect	No effect
B.	Increase	No effect
C.	No effect	Increase
D.	Increase	Increase

assess.AICPA.BEC.cst.proc.mgmt-0004

485. Each of the following should be considered in the selection of appropriate cost drivers for an activity-based costing system **except**

A. Volume-based production.
B. Behavioral effects.
C. Cost of measurement.
D. Degree of correlation.

assess.AICPA.BEC.cst.proc.mgmt-0005

486. A company would most benefit from using an activity-based costing (ABC) system as opposed to a traditional costing system under which of the following conditions?

A. When indirect costs are a high percentage of total costs.
B. When each department within the company has a single activity.
C. When different products use the different activities of the department in the same proportions.
D. When batch-level and product-sustaining costs are immaterial.

Planning Techniques

Budgeting

AICPA.060632BEC

487. What is the required unit production level given the following factors?

	Units
Projected sales	1,000
Beginning inventory	85
Desired ending inventory	100
Prior-year beginning inventory	200

- A. 915.
- B. 1,015.
- C. 1,100.
- D. 1,215.

AICPA.120604BEC

488. Johnson Co., distributor of candles, has reported the following budget assumptions for year 1: No change in candles inventory level; cash disbursement to candle manufacturer, $300,000; target accounts payable ending balance for year 1 is 150% of accounts payable beginning balance; and sales price is set at a markup of 20% of candle purchase price. The candle manufacturer is Johnson's only vendor, and all purchases are made on credit. The accounts payable has a balance of $100,000 at the beginning of year 1. What is the budgeted gross margin for year 1?

- A. $60,000
- B. $70,000
- C. $75,000
- D. $87,500

AICPA.921134BEC-P2-AR

489. Cook Co.'s total costs of operating five sales offices last year were $500,000, of which $70,000 represented fixed costs. Cook has determined that total costs are significantly influenced by the number of sales offices operated. Last year's costs and the number of sales offices can be used as the basis for predicting annual costs. What would be the budgeted costs for the coming year if Cook were to operate seven sales offices?

- A. $700,000.
- B. $672,000.
- C. $614,000.
- D. $586,000.

AICPA.921135BEC-P2-AR

490. Lon Co.'s budget committee is preparing its master budget on the basis of the following projections:

Sales	$2,800,000
Decrease in inventories	70,000
Decrease in accounts payable	150,000
Gross margin	40%

What are Lon's estimated cash disbursements for inventories?

- A. $1,040,000.
- B. $1,200,000.
- C. $1,600,000.
- D. $1,760,000.

AICPA.940537BEC-AR

491. A flexible budget is appropriate for a

	Marketing Budget	Direct Material Usage Budget
A.	No	No
B.	No	Yes
C.	Yes	Yes
D.	Yes	No

Forecasting Techniques

AICPA.081214-SIM

492. In describing the regression equation used for cost prediction, $Y = a + bx$, which of the following is correct?

- A. Y is the total revenue.
- B. a is the variable rate.
- C. a and b are valid for all levels of activity.
- D. a is the total fixed cost.

AICPA.090619BEC-V-A

493. The regression analysis results for ABC Co. are shown as $y = 90x + 45$. The standard error (Sb) is 30 and the coefficient of determination (r^2) is 0.81. The budget calls for the production of 100 units. What is ABC's estimate of total costs?

- A. $3,090.
- B. $4,590.
- C. $9,030.
- D. $9,045.

AICPA.130727BEC

494. In using regression analysis, which measure indicates the extent to which a change in the independent variable explains a change in the dependent variable?

    A. p-value.
    B. r-squared.
    C. Standard error.
    D. t-statistic.

AICPA.920554BEC-P2-AR

495. Box Co. uses regression analysis to estimate the functional relationship between an independent variable (cost driver) and overhead cost.

Assume that the following equation is being used:

$y = A + Bx$.

What is the symbol for the independent variable?

    A. y
    B. x
    C. Bx
    D. A

AICPA.951153BEC-AR

496. Under frost-free conditions, Cal Cultivators expects its strawberry crop to have a $60,000 market value. An unprotected crop subject to frost has an expected market value of $40,000. If Cal protects the strawberries against frost, then the market value of the crop is still expected to be $60,000 under frost-free conditions and $90,000 if there is a frost.

What must be the probability of a frost for Cal to be indifferent to spending $10,000 for frost protection?

    A. .167.
    B. .200.
    C. .250.
    D. .333.

assess.AICPA.BEC.forecst.tech-0003

497. In a regression analysis, the coefficient of determination measures

    A. Economic plausibility.
    B. Goodness of fit.
    C. Independence of residuals.
    D. Independence of variables.

Financial Management

Introduction to Financial Management

AICPA.090531BEC-SIM

498. Which of the following financial management-related areas are considered long-term issues?

	Trade Accounts Payable	Inventories	Capital Budgeting
A.	Yes	Yes	Yes
B.	No	Yes	Yes
C.	No	No	Yes
D.	Yes	No	Yes

AICPA0811600BEC.III.C

499. Financial management involves decisions and activities that deal with

	Short-Term Matters	Long-Term Matters
A.	Yes	Yes
B.	Yes	No
C.	No	Yes
D.	No	No

AICPA0811601BEC.III.C

500. Which one of the following would be considered a long-term financial management activity or concern?

    A. Cash management.
    B. Dividend policy management.
    C. Inventories management.
    D. Accounts payable management.

Answers and Explanations

1. **Answer: B**

   This is an accurate description. Internal control provides reasonable, not absolute, assurance. Internal control investments are limited by cost-benefit trade-offs.

2. **Answer: B**

   This answer is correct because this is an internal report, and it is nonfinancial. (Oil production is not in currency.)

3. **Answer: B**

   Risk assessment is the process of identifying, analyzing, and managing the risks involved in achieving the organization's objectives. Changes related to international exposure, acquisitions, or executive transitions create risks, which must be assessed, prioritized, and responded to.

4. **Answer: C**

   Operations control is not a component of internal control in the COSO model.

5. **Answer: B**

   The control environment is, "...the core or foundation of any system of internal control."

6. **Answer: D**

   Risk assessment is, "...the process of identifying, analyzing, and managing the risks involved in achieving the organization's objectives."

7. **Answer: B**

   Maintaining a safe level of carbon dioxide emissions during production is, in the U.S.A., required for compliance with law or regulation.

8. **Answer: D**

   Remember rat-a-tat-tat (Tat—tone at the top). Tone at the top is critical to internal control; this description evidences a strong tone at the top in this organization.

9. **Answer: A**

   This answer is correct because monitoring involves collecting information to determine that controls are working.

10. **Answer: C**

    If Jiffy Grill has an anonymous hotline set up for this purpose, then this is the best way to communicate this information.

11. **Answer: C**

    According to the COSO principles, Information and communication primarily relate to the quality of information supporting controls, and internal and external communications.

12. **Answer: A**

    This answer is correct because technology development policies and procedures are part of the general controls.

13. **Answer: B**

    This answer is the best Answer Because this is a business risk; it is not a limitation of internal control.

14. **Answer: B**

    Reconciliation of data entry totals with batch control totals will detect errors made by the data entry clerks.

15. **Answer: D**

    Access control software is a preventive control.

16. **Answer: D**

    Restricting access to the computer center is an example of a general control.

17. **Answer: B**

    This is the best answer. Computing overtime requires a calculation (total hours − normal hours = overtime hours) that is independent of the system described. That is, the addition of a time clock and video camera will not directly help in allocating hours worked between normal and overtime hours. In addition, the other answers are, bad choices. Therefore, this is the best answer of the available choices.

18. **Answer: B**

    A code of conduct helps facilitate shared goals and encourages teamwork.

19. **Answer: B**

    Activities of an organization may be outsourced, but the responsibilities never transfer to the outsourced party. Management is never relieved of ultimate responsibility or accountability.

20. **Answer: C**

    This answer is correct because information about social engineering efforts to break into systems should be communicated to all personnel.

21. **Answer: D**

    This answer is correct because support functions are mostly likely to have responsibility for determining system access.

22. **Answer: A**

    This is the primary purpose of monitoring internal control.

23. **Answer: D**

    This is a substantial change; hence it will affect both the assessment of the control baseline and assessment of changes in that baseline (i.e., "change management").

24. **Answer: A**

    COSO indicates that the evaluator must have competence and objectivity. The other answers are incorrect because they do not describe the desired characteristics.

25. **Answer: D**

    Collecting direct information is often costlier than collecting indirect information. Hence, to reduce costs, less important risks are likely to be monitored with indirect information.

26. **Answer: D**

    All of the above are reasons internal controls need to be monitored.

27. **Answer: A**

    This is the best answer. It is the definition of a compensating control.

28. **Answer: D**

    Monitoring is the core, underlying control component in the COSO ERM model. Its position at the foundation is not accidental and reflects the importance of monitoring to achieving strong internal control and effective risk management. Ensuring that internal controls continue to operate effectively is the primary purpose of monitoring.

29. **Answer: C**

    A change control process should include the use of change request forms, an approval process for changes, and appropriate documentation; however, outsourcing is not part of the design for a recommended change control process.

30. **Answer: A**

    This monitoring occurs continuously.

31. **Answer: B**

    The key to recognizing the correctness of this answer is that the question asks who should engage in "evaluating" internal control procedures (not design or implement control procedures). Among the offered choices, an independent internal audit staff, i.e., who report to the board of directors or an audit committee, but not the CFO, are best qualified to monitor and evaluate internal control procedures.

32. **Answer: D**

    "Improving the quality of life" is appropriate for a mission statement since many of such statements include the verb "improving." "We will be known for outstanding …" is a vision statement since the desire to be known for something is often a vision statement aspiration. "We will treat our customers and employees with respect" is a statement of behavior and is therefore best characterized as a statement of core values.

33. **Answer: C**

    A higher performance, in most settings, requires accepting a higher level of risk.

34. **Answer: D**

    Communication is the continual, iterative process of obtaining and sharing information to facilitate and enhance ERM. This function includes reporting on the organization's risk, culture, and performance. This is the component that includes email, board meeting minutes, and reports as important elements.

35. **Answer: C**

    The listed activities are the analysis of the business context, which occurs in the Strategy and Objective-Setting component of ERM.

36. **Answer: A**

    Governance is the allocation of roles, authorities, and responsibilities among stakeholders including attracting, retaining, and developing capable individuals. The listed activities are part of COSO ERM Principle 5, which relates to attracting, retaining, and developing capable individuals.

37. **Answer: D**

    Communication is the continual, iterative process of obtaining and sharing information to facilitate and enhance ERM. This function includes reporting on the organization's risk, culture, and performance. The listed activities are part of COSO ERM Principle 19, which relates to creating communication channels that support ERM.

38. **Answer: A**

    The COSO ERM framework does not list former financial statement auditors as having a potential independence impediment regarding board membership. In addition, the absence of a current business or contractual relationship (as is the case here) is a consideration for a board member's independence. Hence, Jane's independence is not impaired, according to the COSO ERM framework.

39. **Answer: B**

    In a dual board of directors' organization, the management board usually oversees operations while the supervising board oversees strategy.

40. **Answer: D**

    In a risk-aware organization, the culture will be created by a close and careful analysis of the organization's strategy, objectives, and business context.

41. **Answer: B**

    Setting an appropriate tone at the top of both talking and acting consistent with organizational values is important to establishing accountability.

42. **Answer: C**

    Risk appetite is the amount of risk an organization accepts in pursuit of a strategy and value. Risk appetite is focused on strategy and goals. Tolerance sets the boundaries of acceptable performance; it is related to strategy implementation and variation from plans.

43. **Answer: B**

    Yes. Risk appetite may be stated either in words (e.g., "low") or in numbers ("< 3 per year"). Hence, both statements of risk are acceptable.

44. **Answer: C**

    A risk floor is a statement of the minimum amount of risk that an entity desires. A risk ceiling is a statement of the maximum amount of risk that an entity desires.

45. **Answer: A**

    A heat map that is used in assessing the severity of risk plots the likelihood of the risk occurring on the vertical axis against the impact of the risk, should it occur, on the horizontal axis.

46. **Answer: D**

    Target residual risk is the desired risk after implementing a response. Statement I is a statement of target residual risk. Inherent risk is the risk, absent actions to change it. Statement II is a statement of inherent risk. Actual residual risk is the risk that remains after responding to it. Statement III is a statement of actual residual risk.

47. **Answer: D**

    Hedging involves sharing the risk with another party.

48. **Answer: C**

    A relatively small (here 4%) increase in calls to a whistleblower hotline is the least likely event listed to trigger a review and revision to the organization's ERM practices.

49. **Answer: D**

    The organization should review its ERM practices to better understand why it misestimated the risks related to the new product.

50. Answer: A

A review of ERM practices primarily focuses on realized versus targeted risk. This question is tangential to investigating realized versus targeted risks.

51. Answer: B

Staffing data are typically structured; email is unstructured (text).

52. Answer: C

KRIs are usually quantitative and are used to predict risks.

53. Answer: D

The risk profile view would be at the level of a specific unit within the entity (i.e., the human resource function).

54. Answer: C

Having two officers who significantly influence management and operations will not mitigate (i.e., reduce the likelihood) of a management override of controls. Hence, this is the correct answer.

55. Answer: B

Determining reporting procedures is a part of the last (fifth) step of designing a data analytics plan. This procedure is part of determining escalation procedures when a problem is identified in data analysis.

56. Answer: B

This survey question is asking whether a specific fraud risk control is in place. The question relates to selecting, developing, and deploying fraud controls.

57. Answer: D

The company's use of a fraud risk heat map relates to performing a comprehensive fraud risk assessment.

58. Answer: B

SOX requires that a public company's entire audit committee be independent.

59. Answer: C

SOX requires both the CEO and the CFO, but no other officers, to certify the accuracy of their firms' audited financial statements when filed with the SEC.

60. Answer: A

SOX requires the CEO and CFO to certify, among other things, that they are responsible for establishing and maintaining their firm's internal financial controls. But it does not require lie detector tests, or that they promise they have hired an excellent audit firm. Or that they are subject to a code of ethics policing the accuracy of the financial statements.

61. Answer: C

SOX requires the auditors of public companies to audit both their financial statements and their internal controls.

62. Answer: B

SOX required financial experts (who often have accounting experience), but not legal experts or "accounting experts" familiar with the AICPA Code.

63. Answer: B

This is the one of these four choices that need not be certified. It is a fine thing if Mar is a CPA and if her license is active, but neither is required by SOX.

64. Answer: C

SOX requires that every audit committee of a public company have at least one "financial expert" with (a) an understanding of GAAP and financial statements; (b) experience in preparing or auditing financial statements; (c) experience with internal auditing controls; and (d) an understanding of audit committee functions.

65. Answer: D

SOX does not require that a "financial expert" have experience on a compensation committee. It does require that she have an understanding of GAAP and GAAS, an ability to assess the general application of these principles, experience in preparing, auditing, analyzing or evaluating F/S, an understanding of internal controls and procedures for financial reporting, and an understanding of audit committee functions.

66. Answer: C

SOX did create the PCAOB to govern the audit profession.

67. **Answer: D**

This director has breached a fiduciary duty by appropriating a business opportunity (to acquire retail space) for himself or herself.

68. **Answer: C**

"Not interdependent" means that the value of one variable does not depend on the value of another variable. Curves B-B and D-D depict variables that are not interdependent; the value of one variable does not change with a change in the value of the other variable. Conversely, curves A-A and C-C depict variables that are interdependent. For each of these curves, the value of one variable changes as the value of the other changes.

69. **Answer: D**

This statement is not correct. The vertical axis of an economic graph is not referred to as the X axis, but rather as the Y axis. The horizontal axis is referred to as the X axis. (Remember: The letter Y has a vertical stem to it (vertical axis); the letter X has no vertical element.)

70. **Answer: B**

Macroeconomics is concerned with the study of the economic activities of an entire nation (or major sectors of a national economy). It is concerned with such matters as demand/supply, employment/unemployment, inflation/deflation, etc. for an entire country.

71. **Answer: C**

In a free-market economy, government regulation of commerce should be the least significant factor (of those listed) in determining resource allocation and use.

72. **Answer: D**

Initially, a sudden and severe restriction in the availability of consumer credit likely would adversely impact the ability of individuals to provide payment to firms for goods and services. The lack of credit likely would reduce consumer demand, which would then begin to impact other flows.

73. **Answer: A**

Labor (human work, etc.), capital (financial and man-made), and natural resources (land, minerals, etc.) are all economic resources and they are scarce.

74. **Answer: B**

In view of the economic downturn, a decrease in the income of market participants for high-end electronics was probably the direct cause of the decline in demand for Scope's products. A decrease in income is normally associated with a decrease in demand for normal (and "above normal") goods and an increase in demand for inferior goods.

75. **Answer: C**

The demand curve reflects the impact that price has on the amount of a product purchased. A demand curve (or schedule) for a product shows the quantity of a commodity that will be demanded at various prices during a specified time, ceteris paribus (holding variables other than price constant).

76. **Answer: A**

Derived demand is the demand for a good or service that results because it is an input needed in order to provide another good or service for which there is demand. The demand for a good or service is derived from the demand for another good or service. The theory of derived demand explains why an increase in product A increases the demand for resources used to produce product A.

77. **Answer: C**

The statement "quantity supplied is a function of price" means that quantity depends upon price. Therefore, quantity is the dependent variable and price is the independent variable.

78. **Answer: D**

If the supply curve shifts inward (to the left), the same quantity will be provided after the shift as was provided before the shift, only at a higher price.

79. **Answer: D**

An increase in the cost of input factors to the production process will cause the supply curve to shift inward. An increase in input costs will cause the per-unit cost to increase and the supply curve will shift upward and to the left (inward).

80. **Answer: D**

An increase in the market supply of beef (with no change in demand) would result in a new supply and demand equilibrium which reflects an increase in the quantity of beef demanded and a decrease in the price of beef (a movement along the "fixed" demand for beef curve).

81. **Answer: D**

A price ceiling established below the market equilibrium price would be expected to result in a shortage in supply and an excess demand. The price ceiling will limit what can be charged for a good or service, resulting in marginal (high cost) suppliers unable to compete in the market. This will result in a shortage of supply. The shortage in supply, in turn, will result in demand for the good or service (at the "low" controlled price) exceeding what is provided, an excess demand.

82. **Answer: C**

Cross elasticity of demand measures the percentage change in the quantity of a commodity demanded as a result of a given percentage change in the price of another commodity. When the cross elasticity coefficient is greater than zero (0), the goods are substitute goods. A coefficient of 1.5 indicates that as the price of Westco's product increases, the demand for Tower's substitute product will increase by 1.5 times the percentage change in Westco's price. Thus, an increase in Westco's price by 5% would be expected to increase the demand for Tower's product by 7.5% (i.e., 5% × 1.5).

83. **Answer: A**

When a good or service has a high price elasticity of demand the percentage change in quantity demanded is greater than the percentage change in price. When a good or service has many substitutes, a small change in price will result in a greater change in quantity demanded as consumers switch to the substitutes. So, for example, if the price of an item with many substitutes increases, consumers will switch to lower-cost substitutes, reflecting a high price elasticity of demand.

84. **Answer: C**

Since the percentage change in supply (8%) was greater than the percentage change in price (4%), supply is elastic.

85. **Answer: B**

Utility is a measure of satisfaction in economics. Utility is a measure of the satisfaction received

from acquiring a good or service. Thus, to maximize utility is to maximize satisfaction received.

86. **Answer: D**

When total utility is maximized, the marginal utility (MU) of the last dollar spent on each and every item acquired must be the same. Thus, total utility is maximized when: MU of beers/price of beers = MU of pizza/price of pizza. Using the values given: 100 utils/$2.00 = MU of pizza/$10.00. The equation for beers = 100/$2 = 50 utils per dollar. The MU of pizza also must be 50 utils per dollar. Therefore, 50 = MU of pizza × $10 = 500 utils.

87. **Answer: C**

Since total utility is achieve when 3 slices of pizza and 3 bottles of beer are consumed, the marginal unit per dollar must be equal at those quantities of pizza and beer. For that to be true, the price of a slice of pizza must be twice that of the price of a bottle of beer, as computed by the marginal utility of beer divided into the marginal utility of pizza. That calculation would be 60/30, which is 2:1.

88. **Answer: D**

In the long run, a firm can experience increasing returns due to economies of scale. The long-run average cost (LAC) curve is "U" shaped. Where the LAC curve is decreasing, quantity of output increases in greater proportion than the increase in all inputs, primarily due to specialization of labor and equipment. That downward-sloping section of a LAC curve reflects increasing returns to scale.

89. **Answer: B**

Since, by definition, fixed costs do not change with changes in output over the relevant range of production, the more units produced, the lower the average fixed cost. Simply put, more units are being produced for a fixed cost. Therefore, the average fixed cost decreases continuously over the relevant range of production. It is not "U-shaped."

90. **Answer: C**

Since output increases in lesser proportion (75%) than inputs (100%), there are decreasing returns to scale; the returns from increasing the scale of operations in the long-run are less than proportionate to the inputs incurred in increasing the scale of operations.

This is a long-run concept in which all inputs are considered variable and primarily result from problems (communication, coordination, etc.) associated with managing very large-scale operations.

91. **Answer: C**

The extent of competition in the market is central to determining the nature of market structure. Perfect competition occupies one end of a conceptual market structure continuum and perfect monopoly—the absence of competition—occupies the other end.

92. **Answer: B**

Socialism is a broad set of economic theories that advocate state or collective ownership and administration of the means of production and distribution of goods consistent with a command economy, not a free-market economy.

93. **Answer: A**

When the market price is less than a firm's average variable cost, the firm should cease to produce and exit the market. At this price-to-cost relationship, each unit the firm produces does not cover the variable cost to produce the product and total losses increase with every unit produced.

94. **Answer: A**

A perfectly competitive financial market assumes that there are a large number of independent buyers and sellers, each of whom is too small to separately affect the price of a commodity. Individual traders in such a market would be "price takers" who may sell any quantity of its commodity at market price.

95. **Answer: D**

A monopolistic firm that produces at the quantity that maximizes revenue will use resources inefficiently and will have a higher price than a firm in perfect competition. The inefficient use of resources and the price that is higher than it would be in perfect competition result because the monopolistic firm faces a downward-sloping demand curve.

96. **Answer: B**

A natural monopoly results from conditions in which there are increasing returns to scale, such that a single firm can produce at a lower cost

than two or more firms. Typically, fixed costs are extremely high, making it inefficient for a second firm to enter the market.

97. **Answer: B**

Under monopolistic competition, there will be a greater variety of products produced at a higher unit cost than under perfect competition. Under perfect competition, there are a large number of buyers and sellers, each of which is too small to separately affect the price of the good or service, selling a homogeneous good or service, and entry into (or exit from) the market is easy. Since each firm must accept the price set by the market (be a "price taker"), a firm's marginal revenue (MR) is equal to the price (P) it can charge. Optimum production output occurs where MR = marginal cost (MC) = P. If firms are making a profit at that level of output, more firms will enter the market, which will increase market supply and drive market price down so that each firm just breaks even. In a monopolistically competitive market, a large number of providers sell differentiated products or services for which there are close substitutes. Because there is product differentiation, the MR and demand (D) curves have downward slopes, with the MR below D. As in perfect competition, optimum output occurs where MR = MC. At that level of output (MR = MC), P will be greater than MC and greater than P under perfect competition. Therefore, a monopolistically competitive industry produces a greater variety of products at a higher cost per unit than would occur in perfect competition.

98. **Answer: B**

While a firm in monopolistic competition can make an economic profit in the short run, it cannot do so in the long run because new firms will enter the market and/or consumers will switch to substitute products.

99. **Answer: A**

The demand curve in monopolistic competition is negatively sloped—the lower the price, the greater the quantity demanded.

100. **Answer: C**

Oligopolistic firms are less like to collude when the general economic conditions are recessionary. In a recessionary period, firms are likely to face decreased demand and excess productive capacity. Therefore, they are more likely to unilaterally reduce their sales price in an effort to increase market share at the expense of other firms in the industry. There is more incentive not to agree on price or profits in an attempt to gain market share to offset decreased general demand.

101. **Answer: A**

Collusive pricing occurs when the few firms in an oligopolistic market (or industry) conspire to set the price at which a good or service will be provided. Such collusion typically is carried out to establish a price higher than would exist under normal competition. Overt collusive pricing is illegal in the U.S.A.

102. **Answer: A**

An industry or market that meets all of the characteristics of perfect competition is virtually nonexistent in the U.S. (or in other developed market systems). While some industries or markets possess some of the characteristics of perfect competition, none possesses all of the essential characteristics of perfect competition.

For example, perfect competition assumes the product or service is perfectly homogeneous, such that there are no differences in size, quality, style, or other features and, therefore, no reason to advertise in order to compete.

103. **Answer: A**

As the term implies, price discrimination is a pricing strategy that charges customers in different market segments different prices for the same or largely the same product or service. When a market has distinct segments (i.e., buyers that are of fairly distinct types), suppliers are better able to charge different prices to different buyer types (market segments) for the same or essentially the same good or service. For example, it is common for pharmaceutical companies to charge different prices for the same drug to different geographic market segments. As a consequence, U.S. consumers pay almost twice what Europeans pay for the same drugs.

104. **Answer: C**

Elasticity of demand is the issue that is least likely to be studied in macroeconomics, as it is concerned with the effects of a change in price on the demand for an individual good or service and not with the activity or outcome of an entire economy.

105. **Answer: A**

In a macroeconomic free-market flow model, leakages result when income is used for purposes other than domestic consumption. Both savings and taxes (as well as payments for imports) are uses of income for purposes other than domestic consumption.

106. **Answer: D**

In a macroeconomic free-market flow model, injections are the sources of amounts added to domestic production that do not result from domestic consumption expenditures, including government spending, government subsidiaries, investment spending, and amounts received from exports, but not amounts paid for imports.

107. **Answer: B**

The individual's marginal propensity to save is 0.4. This rate is calculated as the change in savings divided by the change in income, or $700 − $500 = $200/$3,500 − $3,000 = $500, or $200/$500 = 0.40.

108. **Answer: C**

In order to reach full employment, gross domestic product needs to increase by $.1 trillion (i.e., $1.3 trillion @ full employment − $1.2 trillion @ current = $.1 trillion shortfall). Because of the multiplier effect, additional government expenditures needed to increase gross domestic product by that amount is $20 billion. The formula is: Multiplier Effect = Initial Change in Spending $\times$ (1/(1 − MPC)) Where: Initial Change in Spending = X, and substituting known values: $.1T = X \times [1/(1−.8)]$ [NOTE: .1T = 100B.]; therefore:

$100B =	X × [1/.2]
$100B =	X × 5
X =	$100B/5
X =	$20B

A $20B increase in government expenditures would result in $100 billion increase in gross domestic product.

109. **Answer: B**

A federal deficit results when federal payments are greater than federal revenue for a period. A decrease in tax revenues and an increase in entitlement payments does imply a deficit, since those changes would reduce revenues while increasing payments.

110. **Answer: C**

Since labor is an economic resource, a decrease in labor would shift the aggregate supply curve inward (i.e., reduce aggregate supply).

111. **Answer: B**

An increase in the minimum wage rate would be an increase in the cost of economic resources (labor), which would shift the aggregate supply curve inward—a reduction in supply.

112. **Answer: A**

A reduction in aggregate supply will shift the supply curve to the left, resulting in a lower quantity of output at a higher price.

113. **Answer: D**

Potential GDP is the maximum amount of various goods and services an economy can produce at a given time with available technology and full utilization of economic resources. The point at which the aggregate demand and aggregate supply curves intersect is equilibrium—the real output (and price level) for an economy. The real output may be at, above, or below potential GDP (output).

114. **Answer: A**

An increase in the value of the Chinese RMB relative to the U.S. dollar would most likely increase aggregate demand in the U.S. An increase in the value of the Chinese RMB relative to the U.S. dollar would make Chinese goods more expensive in the U.S. and U.S. goods less expensive in China. As a consequence, fewer goods would be bought from China by U.S. consumers and more goods would be bought from the U.S. by Chinese consumers. Furthermore, U.S. consumers might also buy (substitute) more U.S. goods for the now more expensive Chinese goods.

115. **Answer: B**

A higher level of output reflects a shift in the supply curve to the right. This would result in an increase in quantity of output and a decrease in price.

116. **Answer: B**

A higher level of output reflects a shift in the supply curve to the right. If a Keynesian supply curve is assumed and demand is at full employment, this would result in an increase in quantity of output and a decrease in price.

117. **Answer: B**

The natural rate of unemployment is achieved when there is no cyclical unemployment. The reasons for unemployment fall into one of four categories: (1) Frictional unemployment, (2) structural unemployment, (3) seasonal unemployment, and (4) cyclical unemployment. The natural rate of unemployment is measured as the sum of frictional, structural, and seasonal unemployment. Cyclical unemployment is not included in the definition or measurement of the natural rate of unemployment. At the peak of a business cycle, the level of employment is at its highest, and there would be no unemployment caused by a lack of business activity. Therefore, at the peak of the peak of the business cycle, there would be only frictional, structural, and seasonal unemployment, the components of natural unemployment.

118. **Answer: B**

A product that is in the finished goods inventory at the end of one year (Year 1) should be included in total in the GDP for that year. Since the product does not require further processing before being sold, it should be included in GDP of the year in which it was "finished," regardless of when it is sold.

119. **Answer: C**

National income is the total payments for economic resources included in the production of all goods and services. During the recessionary phase of a business cycle, actual national income is typically less than potential national income as a result of decreased demand, which is characteristic of the recessionary phase of a business cycle and the resulting decrease in payments for goods and services.

120. **Answer: C**

The rate of unemployment caused by changes in the composition of employment opportunities over time is referred to as the structural unemployment rate. Specifically, structural unemployment results from those members of the labor force who are not employed because their prior types of jobs have been greatly reduced or eliminated and/or because they lack the skills needed for available jobs.

121. **Answer: D**

There could be official full employment when there is structural, frictional, and/or seasonal unemployment. Only cyclical unemployment is considered in the official measure of full employment.

122. **Answer: C**

Short-term unemployment is not a cause of unemployment and is not a type or category of unemployment used to describe the causes of or reasons for unemployment. Technological advances cause structural unemployment.

123. **Answer: B**

This sequence of business cycle phases is correct. A peak is a point in the economic cycle that marks the end of rising aggregate output and the beginning of a decline in output. A recession is a period during which aggregate output is decreasing. A trough is a point in the economic cycle that marks the end of a decline in aggregate output and the beginning of an increase in output. A recovery is a period during which aggregate output is increasing.

124. **Answer: D**

The increases and decreases in economic activity associated with the business cycle are less likely to directly affect the healthcare industry than most other industries.

Since healthcare generally is not discretionary, it is less likely to be affected by fluctuations in the business cycle.

125. **Answer: C**

Business cycles are the cumulative fluctuations (up and down) in aggregate real GDP of a country and generally last for two or more years. While these increases and decreases in real GDP tend to recur over time, there is no consistent pattern of length (duration) or magnitude (intensity) of the cycles.

126. **Answer: A**

Output will increase to meet the increase in aggregate demand, which is the basis for demand-pull inflation.

127. **Answer: D**

The real value of the $1,030 is $1,009.80. It is calculated by reducing the principal and

interest for the rate of inflation, or $1,030/1.02 = $1,009.80.

128. **Answer: D**

The correct formula to compute the percentage changes for account balances is (Current balance − Prior balance) / Prior balance. The numerator computes the change in amount from the prior year balance to the current year balance and the use of the prior year's balance in the denominator determines the percentage change from the prior year's balance.

129. **Answer: C**

Depreciation does not reflect current fixed-asset replacement costs. Depreciation is the systematic and rational allocation of long-term assets over the period benefited. Thus, depreciation (expense) reflects the portion of the historical cost of the asset allocated to the current period. Since the asset may have been acquired many periods ago, during a period of inflation the current allocation will reflect the old price of the asset, not the current price (replacement cost) of the asset.

130. **Answer: C**

A reduction in monetary growth would be expected to increase interest rates as the quantity of money in circulation (supply) is reduced. Higher interest rates will cause a decrease in business investments and consumer purchases of durable goods due to the higher cost of buying on credit. Decreases in business investments and consumer spending on durable goods would be expected to lower GDP growth.

131. **Answer: A**

Through its exercise of monetary policy, the Federal Reserve (the Fed) can take actions intended to expand or contract the economy. An expansionary policy would serve to increase spending, demand, employment, and other economic measures. By purchasing federal securities (through its Open Market Committee), the Fed would put more cash into the economy by providing cash to the selling investors (e.g., banks, etc.). Increasing cash (the money supply) typically serves to stimulate the economy. In addition, lowering the discount rate (the interest rate the Fed charges for short-term loans to banks) would reduce the cost of borrowing by banks, thus increasing their ability to make loans for consumption and investment purposes.

132. Answer: C

A reduction in the discount rate would increase the money supply. The discount rate is the interest rate banks pay when borrowing from a Federal Reserve Bank (the "Fed"). By reducing the discount rate, the cost of borrowing is reduced and banks increase lending, which increases the money supply.

133. Answer: C

Comparative advantage exists when one entity has the ability to produce a good or service at a lower opportunity cost than the opportunity cost of the good or service for another entity. Comparative advantage is the basis for international trade. When a country has comparative advantage in the production of a good or provision of a service, it should produce that good or provide that service to other countries in exchange for the goods/services for which the other country has a comparative advantage. The total output of two or more countries will be greatest when each produces the goods or services for which it has the lowest opportunity cost (the principle of comparative advantage).

134. Answer: C

Protection of manufacturing capabilities is not typically one of the reasons a U.S. entity would engage in international economic activity. Engaging in international activity generally would result in a U.S. entity either buying manufactured goods abroad or moving its manufacturing facilities abroad to benefit from lower labor cost. The results would be a decline in U.S. manufacturing capabilities.

135. Answer: C

The concept of comparative advantage in international business activity is based on differences in relative opportunity costs. Comparative advantage is the ability of one economic entity (nation) to produce a good or service at a lower opportunity cost than another entity (nation).

136. Answer: A

In the context of international economics, "dumping" is the sale of a product in a foreign market at a price that is either lower than is charged in the domestic market or lower than the firm's production cost. Although Alpha Company's mill price to foreign customers ($59) is not lower than its price to domestic customers ($56), its price to foreign customers ($59) is lower than its production cost ($60).

137. Answer: D

The import of asset from foreign countries would be accomplished by the transfer of capital from the United States to sellers in foreign countries that would decrease the capital accounting, which would reduce the balance of payments for the United States.

138. Answer: A

The imposition of tariffs has the effects of increasing the cost of the good or service on which the tariff is placed and protecting domestic producers of the good or service from foreign competition. The result most likely will be an increase in production by domestic producers of the good/service in the protected domestic industries, creating an increased employment demand in those industries. Concurrently, exports are likely to decline as affected foreign countries retaliate by imposing import tariffs or other restrictions on goods/services of the country that initially imposed tariffs on its goods/services. This will cause a decrease in employment in export industries. Thus, the net effect is most likely to be a movement of domestic workers from export industries to industries protected by the tariff.

139. Answer: B

There is no "non-current account" in the balance of payments statement. This title is used in financial accounting for private (and other) entities to refer to an account that is not expected to be settled within one year or within the operating cycle of the entity, whichever is longer, but it is not used in connection with accounting and reporting of the U.S. international balance of payments. The other three account titles listed are the components of the U.S. balance of payments statement.

140. Answer: A

If the real rates of interest are the same, the country with the higher nominal interest rate is expected to experience a higher rate of inflation. A higher rate of inflation is associated with the devaluing of a currency, so the currency of the country with the higher nominal interest rate (Country A) likely will sell at a forward discount relative to the currency of the other country (Country B).

141. **Answer: C**

Except in countries that strictly control their exchange rates, generally such rates are determined by the supply and demand for a currency in the foreign exchange market.

142. **Answer: A**

A lack of equilibrium in the balance of payment results when a country has imports from abroad and investments made abroad that are different than (greater than or less than) exports to other countries and investments made in the country (i.e., "outflows" are different than "inflows"). That imbalance causes the relative demand for the currency of each country to be different. Fluctuating exchange rates permit these changing demands to be realized, which enables a return to equilibrium. For example, with a U.S. deficit in the balance of payments, the U.S. demand for foreign currencies will exceed the foreign currencies provided by foreign currency inflows. As a result, there will be an increase in demand for foreign currencies relative to the U.S. dollar, and freely fluctuating exchange rates will enable the value of the dollar relative to other currencies (i.e., the exchange rate) to fall and help move the balance of payments back into equilibrium.

143. **Answer: A**

The total return from a capital investment in a foreign operation is the sum of the return from the investment and the gain or loss (return) resulting from changes in the currency exchange rate between the two countries. If the U.S. dollar declines in value relative to the foreign country in which the capital investment is located, the currency of that foreign country will convert to more dollars when repatriated to the U.S. than before the decline in value. The resulting gain on conversion from the foreign currency to dollars would serve to increase the total return rate on the investment and thus compensate for a lower return on the investment per se.

144. **Answer: B**

The percentage change is computed by first converting the initial investment to its foreign currency value at the date of investment; that is: $20,000,000 × 2.57 = 51,400,000 FC units. Next, the dollar value of the investment is determined after the change in exchange rate; that is: 51,400,000 FC / 3.15 = $16,317.400. Then the percentage change in the dollar value of the investment is determined; that is: $16,317,400

/ $20,000,000 = 81.59%. Finally, since the dollar value of the investment after the change is exchange rate is only 81.59% of its prior value, there is a loss of 100.00% − 81.6% = 18.4% (decrease). [Alternative percentage calculation: $20,000,000 − $16,317,400 = $3,682,600 / $20,000,000 = 18.4% (decrease).]

145. **Answer: A**

Since the American importer will be paying in British pounds, it would want an option to buy pounds in the future, thus, it would buy a call option to acquire British pounds.

146. **Answer: A**

Since the tax rate is lower in Country A, the multinational parent company should maximize the transfer price between Country A and Country B. For every dollar of transfer price recognized in Country A, as opposed to being recognized in Country B, the multinational will benefit by .10 in taxes saved.

147. **Answer: C**

Transfer pricing is the determination of the amounts at which transactions between affiliated entities will be recorded. The issue of transfer pricing has special significance when the affiliated entities are located in different countries.

148. **Answer: B**

Costs incurred by the buying affiliate is not a common basis for establishing a transfer price between affiliated entities. The transfer price would constitute an element of cost in determining (total) costs incurred by the buying affiliate; costs to the buying affiliate would not establish the transfer price paid by the buying affiliate.

149. **Answer: B**

The objective of the World Bank is to promote general economic development, especially in developing countries, primarily by leading for infrastructure, agricultural, education, and similar needs.

150. **Answer: D**

Establishing procedures for collection of international debt is not a purpose of the General Agreement on Tariffs and Trade (GATT). GATT has as its primary purposes the liberalizing and encouraging international trade by eliminating tariffs, subsidies, import quotas, and other trade barriers, to harmonize intellectual property laws and to reduce transportation costs.

151. **Answer: C**

Foreign direct investment would not include investments in foreign bonds, but would include investments in foreign production facilities. Foreign **direct** investment involves investments in non-monetary assets (e.g., property, plant, equipment, etc.) in a foreign location.

152. **Answer: C**

Both statements are correct. International trade has been facilitated by regional trade agreements (e.g., NAFTA, EEU, etc.) (Statement I) and benefits both exporters and importers (Statement II).

153. **Answer: A**

Both a country's imports and exports enter into the determination of that country's gross domestic product. Specifically, it is **net** exports (exports minus imports) that enter into the determination of gross domestic product.

154. **Answer: A**

China is the world's largest exporter of goods/services, followed by German and the United States.

155. **Answer: A**

Outsourcing of goods may involve acquiring either raw materials or final (finished) goods (or intermediate goods).

156. **Answer: C**

A firm that outsources the production of a good to a foreign supplier is least likely to face market risk, i.e., the risk that the value of an asset will decline as a result of a decline in general economic conditions.

157. **Answer: B**

Including an arbitration clause in the contract with the foreign supplier would mitigate the risk associated with outsourcing by providing a predetermined mechanism for resolving differences between the buyer and the supplier (Statement II). Negotiating for payment to the foreign supplier to be made in the foreign currency would not mitigate the risk because it would subject the domestic buyer to foreign currency exchange risk, i.e., the risk that changes in the exchange rate between the currencies will increase the cost of acquiring goods (Statement I).

158. **Answer: A**

Capital markets facilitate the trading of both stocks and bonds.

159. **Answer: C**

If the dollar strengthens against a foreign currency, an investment denominated in that currency would result in fewer dollars; if the dollar weakens against a foreign currency, borrowing in that currency would cost more dollars, as more dollars would be required to service and repay the debt.

160. **Answer: C**

Brazil has not had a decline in share of worldwide output over the last 40 years. During that period, Brazil's share of worldwide output increased from about 2% to about 4%.

161. **Answer: B**

Mexico is not one of the world's largest exporters of goods and services. The largest exporters are China, Germany, the U.S., and Japan, in that order.

162. **Answer: C**

The U.S. exports about 10% of worldwide exports.

163. **Answer: A**

A company can reduce the potential loss from expropriation of a foreign subsidiary by the local government by financing the subsidiary with local-country capital. If the company uses local-country capital (e.g., borrowing from a local bank), in the event of expropriation by the local government, it can default on the borrowing, thus offsetting the unpaid debt against the loss from asset expropriation.

164. **Answer: A**

Government-imposed trade barriers may restrict either imports or exports (or both). While trade barriers are often thought of as restricting imports, governments also impose trade barriers to restrict exports. Export restrictions normally are imposed to protect technology or to preclude countries from receiving certain goods.

165. **Answer: D**

A foreign subsidiary is most likely to give an entity greatest control over an international business activity. Since a parent entity has controlling ownership of a subsidiary, under normal circumstances, it has complete control of the activities of a subsidiary.

166. **Answer: C**

Acquiring a pre-existing foreign entity does not assure synergies between the acquiring entity and the acquired entity. Studies have shown that most mergers and acquisitions to not result in creating value for the acquiring entity.

167. **Answer: C**

First-to-market is not one of the three generic strategies identified by Porter. The three generic strategies he identified are cost leadership, differentiation, and focus.

168. **Answer: B**

Evaluation and control is concerned with the measurement of post-performance characteristics to determine whether an entity is achieving its strategic objectives and to implement changes as needed to achieve objectives.

169. **Answer: A**

The five forces framework developed by Michael Porter is used for determining the nature, operating attractiveness, and probable long-run profitability of a competitive industry.

170. **Answer: C**

PEST is the acronym for "Political, Economic, Social, and Technological," which are the characteristics of a nation or region considered in macro-environmental analysis.

171. **Answer: A**

The political factors considered in PEST analysis are concerned with the nature of the political environment and the ways and the extent to which a government intervenes in an economy. The political environment includes, among other factors, labor law, environmental law, and other relevant aspects of law.

172. **Answer: D**

Climate conditions is not a factor that is explicitly included in PEST analysis, but is explicitly included in PESTEL analysis. In PESTEL analysis, climate conditions would be part of the environmental (the second "E") factors considered.

173. **Answer: D**

If customers have strong brand loyalty, the competitive threat in an industry would not be higher because customers would be less likely to switch to substitute goods or services.

174. **Answer: C**

When information about the sources of the product is widely available, customers are able to comparison shop for the lowest price and are, therefore, more likely to be able to affect price.

175. **Answer: C**

The highest intensity of rivalry should be in an industry with a high fixed cost structure, in which producers seek to operate at full capacity, and a low degree of product differentiation, which results in products having many substitutes.

176. **Answer: B**

The possibility of new regulations in the operating environment would be considered an external threat to the entity. New regulations may restrict or otherwise change the way an entity in the regulated industry operates and reduce its competitive position.

177. **Answer: C**

Decreases in international trade barriers would not be a possible threat to an entity. Decreased trade barriers may make it easier for the entity to purchase goods from foreign suppliers (imports) or sell to foreign buyers (exports), either of which would be an opportunity, not a threat.

178. **Answer: C**

The W/T intersection in a SWOT matrix shows the relationship between an entity's internal weaknesses and the threats in the external environment. The threats pose the greatest risk to the entity because its weaknesses are in the same areas as the threats.

179. **Answer: C**

Market monopoly is not a generic strategy identified by Porter. Porter identified three generic strategies: cost leadership, differentiation, and market focus.

180. **Answer: D**

As strengths, a cost leadership entity typically has both significant capital invested in production and other assets and an efficient distribution system. These and other characteristics are necessary to maintain low cost and a cost competitive advantage.

181. **Answer: C**

The strength and dedication of an entity's marketing function is not critical for an entity that follows the cost leadership strategy, but is critical to an entity that follows the differentiation strategy. Entities that follow the cost leadership strategy compete on price. When following the differentiation strategy, an entity must be able to convey to its customers and potential customers the qualities that make the good or service distinctive and generally worth a higher price than other goods/services.

182. **Answer: A**

Strategic goals should be both measurable (capable of being measured) and time-bound (accomplished by a specified time).

183. **Answer: C**

PEST analysis is a form of macro-environmental analysis and is primarily concerned with where an entity should operate and SWOT is a form of micro-environmental analysis and is primarily concerned how an entity should operate.

184. **Answer: B**

The original cost of the old machine should not be considered in deciding whether or not to replace it with a new machine. The original cost of the old machine is a sunk cost, i.e., a cost that has been incurred in the past, cannot be changed by current decisions, and is irrelevant to making current and future replacement decisions.

185. **Answer: C**

The purchase price of the new van and disposal price of the old van are the (only) relevant costs in making the decision whether to replace the delivery van. The other factors given in the facts are not relevant. The purchase price of the old van and related depreciation are sunk costs and the gain that would be recognized on the sale of the van ($12,000 − $10,000 = $2,000) would be incorporated in the disposal price (selling price) of the old van.

186. **Answer: A**

The use of a company-wide cost of capital to evaluate new capital investments will result in high-risk divisions over-investing in new projects and low-risk divisions under-investing in new projects. Because the company has multiple operating divisions, each having unique risk attributes and related capital costs, the use of a company-wide cost of capital to evaluate new capital investments applies a common, average hurdle rate to all projects, regardless of the risk or cost of capital of the particular division for which the capital investment is being considered. Thus, for example, a high-risk division will use the company-wide average cost of capital that will be less than the cost of capital appropriate for its risk and separate cost of capital. Similarly, a low-risk division will use a cost of capital that is greater than the cost of capital appropriate for its risk and separate cost of capital.

187. **Answer: B**

As a result of selecting project X with a net present value of $1,000,000, the company gives up the opportunity to select project Y with a net present value of $750,000. Thus, $750,000 is the opportunity cost associated with selecting project X.

188. **Answer: A**

This question is intended to test a candidate's understanding of the conceptual relationships between present values of single amounts and present values of annuities, and the impact of length of time on present value amounts. Getting the correct answer does not require (or expect) the actual calculation of present values for each of the four choices. Here is the logic:

1. Recognize that all of the choices are for the same amount, $100. Therefore, the amount of the principal will not create a difference in present values for the choices.

2. Next, notice that choices A, B, and D are for annuities; choice C is for a single amount to be received in four years, longer than choices B and

D, and as long as choice A. Since the present value of a single amount has to be less than the present value of a series of equal amounts due within the same or less time, choice C cannot result in the highest present value.

3. Next, since choices A, B, and D are all for annuities of the same amount, the longer the annuity, the higher the present value. Choices B and D are for three years; choice A is for four years.

4. Therefore, choice A will result in the highest present value.

189. **Answer: C**

Since only present values of an annuity factor are given, the correct answer can be determined only by converting the values given into two annuities. An annuity is a series of equal payments. The given values are:

$30,000 for years 1 and 2, and $20,000 for year 3.

Those values are not equal for every year (therefore not an annuity), so the annuity factors given cannot be used with those values (as given). But, they can be converted into two series of equal payments comprised of:

$20,000 for years 1, 2 and 3, and $10,000 for years 1 and 2.

Those two cash flow streams would look like:

Year	Stream 1	Stream 2	Stream 3
Year 1	$20,000	$10,000	= $30,000
Year 2	$20,000	$10,000	= $30,000
Year 3	$20,000		= $20,000

Note that now there are two series, each of equal amounts, but which total to the same amounts as the values given. The present value of an annuity for 3 years can now be applied to $20,000 and the present value of an annuity for 2 years can be applied to $10,000. The results would be:

(1) $10,000 annuity for two years: $10,000(1.65)	$16,500
(2) $20,000 annuity for three years $20,000(2.32)	46,400
Total present value	$62,900

190. **Answer: C**

Option B, the present value of a $1,400 annual annuity for 10 years, provides the greater net present value, $7,910. That present value is computed as: $1,400 × 5.650 = $7,910. The present value of option A is $20,000 × .322 = $6,440, which is less than the present value of option B, $7,910.

191. **Answer: B**

A yield curve shows the relationship between time to maturity and bond interest rates.

192. **Answer: C**

The effective cost of the loan (i.e., the effective interest rate on the loan) is determined as the annual dollar cost of the loan divided by the net useable proceeds of the loan. The annual dollar cost is the principal multiplied by the annual rate, or $200,000 × .12 = $24,000. The net useable proceeds of the loan is the principal amount less the amount of the compensating balance that must be maintained with the bank, or $200,000 − ($200,000 × .20) = $200,000 − $40,000 = $160,000. Therefore, the effective cost of the loan is $24,000/$160,000 = .15 (or 15%).

193. **Answer: A**

The market rate of interest on a one-year U.S. Treasury bill would be 3%. Notice that the risk-free rate of interest and the various premiums are for the general market rate of interest, not for the rate on a one-year U.S. Treasury bill. Treasury bills are considered risk free in an environment where zero inflation is expected. Therefore, the market rate of interest on a one-year U.S. Treasury bill would be the risk-free rate plus the inflation premium (for the expected rate of inflation during the life of the security), or 2% + 1% = 3%. One-year U.S. Treasury bills are considered free of default risk, liquidity risk (because there is a very large and active secondary market for T-bills), and maturity risk (because they are for only one year).

194. **Answer: B**

These terms would provide the desired 12% annual interest rate. The interest rate associated with discount terms is computed as:

[Discount Rate/Principal] × [1/(Length of discount period/365)]; where:

Principal = Amount after discount

Length of discount period = Difference between discount date and net date

Using the facts in this question: [.01/.99] × [1/(30/365)] = .0101 × (365/30) =

.0101 × 12.16 = 12.28 (or 12% rounded) annual interest rate, the correct answer.

(NOTE: An easier and quicker approximation can be made by dividing the discount period into the days in a year, or 45 − 15 = 30 days; 365/30 = 12.1, and multiplying that by the discount amount = 12.1 × .01 = .121 (or 12% rounded), the correct answer.)

195. **Answer: B**

Level 1 and level 2 inputs are based on observable inputs, but level 3 inputs are not based on observable inputs.

196. **Answer: C**

Converting future amounts to current amounts is an income approach to determining fair value under the U.S. GAAP framework. Specifically, the use of discounted cash flows to determine the current value of those flows is an example of the income approach to determining fair value.

197. **Answer: A**

The market approach to determining value will most likely provide the best evidence of fair value. The market approach is based on using prices or other relevant information generated by actual market transactions for assets or liabilities that are identical or comparable to those being valued.

198. **Answer: A**

Level 1 inputs are quoted prices in active markets for identical assets or liabilities. Either equity securities or debt securities that are traded in an active market could be valued using the prices established in those markets.

199. **Answer: D**

Level 1 inputs in the U.S. GAAP hierarchy are based exclusively on observable quoted prices in active markets, not on unobservable inputs. Both level 2 and level 3 can include inputs not directly observable for the item being valued.

200. **Answer: A**

Level 2 inputs in the U.S. GAAP hierarchy of inputs for fair value determination include quoted prices in active markets for similar (but not identical) assets or liabilities as well as quoted prices for identical or similar assets or liabilities in inactive markets.

201. **Answer: B**

Beta measures the volatility of a stock relative to the market. In general, beta measures volatility of an asset against the asset class of the asset being valued. For stock, the asset class would be the market in which the stock is traded.

202. **Answer: A**

An investment's beta measures the investment's systematic risk; it shows how the value of an investment changes with changes in the entire class of similar investments. Systematic risk is the uncertain inherent in the entire market; it cannot be avoided through diversification.

203. **Answer: C**

The capital asset pricing model does consider the time value of money through the use of the risk-free rate of return. Therefore, failure to consider the time value of money is not a limitation of the model.

204. **Answer: A**

Failing to consider the probability that the option will be exercised is not a limitation of the basic Black-Sholes option pricing model. The basic Black-Scholes option pricing model does consider the probability (likelihood) that the option will be exercised.

205. **Answer: D**

The Black-Scholes option pricing model does not accommodate options when the price of the underlying stock changes significantly and rapidly. The Black-Scholes model assumes that the stock for which the option is being valued increases in small increments.

206. **Answer: A**

The stock has an 80% chance of selling at $72.50 at the end of the option period. That is $12.50 above the option price. The stock has a 20% chance of selling at $65.00 at the end of the option period. That is $5.00 above the option price. Therefore, the value of the option is:

[(.80 × $12.50) + (.20 × $ 5.00)]/1.10, or

[($10.00) + ($1.00)]/1.10, or

$11.00/1.10 = $10.00 × 100 shares = $1,000

207. **Answer: D**

The price/earnings (P/E) ratio is computed as the market price of the stock divided by the earnings per share (EPS). Note that both values are on a per share basis and the resulting calculation shows the relationship between the price of a share of stock in the market and the earnings for each share of stock.

208. **Answer: A**

The asset approach values a business by adding (summing) the values of the individual assets that comprise the business. When a business is losing money and is going to be sold in a distressed sale, the value of the individual assets is a better basis for valuing the business than would be other methods of valuation (e.g., market approach or income approach).

209. **Answer: C**

All three types of risk can be hedged.

210. **Answer: B**

Selling Treasury notes futures contract would hedge the risk of increases in the short-term interest rates. If the interest rates increase, the value of the Treasury notes contract will decline, which would enable the firm to acquire the notes at the new lower value and sell them at the higher futures contract price, resulting in a gain. The gain would serve to offset the effects of an increase in short-term interest rates on the variable rate financing.

211. **Answer: A**

Buying pounds in the forward exchange market would hedge a decrease in the dollar against the pound. Buying pounds now through a forward contract would lock in the dollar cost of the pounds need to pay the obligation when it comes due and, thus, protect the American importer against depreciation of the dollar against the pound.

212. **Answer: A**

Risk is the possibility of loss or other unfavorable result that derives from the uncertainty implicit in future outcomes. In the context of a portfolio of projects, it is the uncertain outcome associated with any project.

213. **Answer: B**

The risk-free rate of interest, as the term implies, is the interest that would be charged on a borrowing that carried no risks (e.g., of default, inflation, etc.). This interest is required by lenders, not to cover risks, but to compensate the lender for deferring use of the funds by making an investment.

214. **Answer: C**

The expected payback period is computed as the length of time needed for net cash flows to recover the initial cash investment in a project. Since the payback period is given, that period multiplied by the annual net cash inflow will result the cost of the new machine. The annual revenue is $35,000 and the annual cash expenses are $3,000, which is determined as the total operating expenses less the amount of depreciation expense included (since it is a non-cash expense). Thus, the annual net cash flow is $35,000 − $3,000 = $32,000 × 5.2 = $166,400, the correct answer.

215. **Answer: A**

The payback period method determines how many years would be required to recover the initial project investment cost. It is calculated as:

Payback = investment cost/annual cash savings.

For the facts given, the calculation would be: Payback period = $5,000/$2,000 = 2.5 years.

216. **Answer: B**

The profitability index approach to capital project evaluation is primarily concerned with the relative economic ranking of projects by taking into account the cost of a project as well as with its net present value.

217. **Answer: A**

The discounted payback period approach to assessing a capital project determines the number of years (or other periods) needed to recover the initial cash investment in the project and compares the resulting time with a preestablished maximum payback period. Because the discounted payback period approach determines only the length of time required to recover the initial investment, it does not consider the results after the payback period; it ignores cash flows received after the payback period.

218. **Answer: B**

The discounted payback period approach does determine the number of periods required for the discounted cash inflows of a project to equal its discounted cash outflows.

219. **Answer: C**

The payback (period) approach determines the number of years (or other periods) needed to recover the initial cash investment in a project. It is calculated as the net investment in the project divided by the annual cash (net) inflows of the project. It uses undiscounted cash flows (i.e., does not consider the time value of money) and considers the project cash flows only up to the point at which the initial investment is recovered (i.e., does not measure whether or not the project will be profitable over its entire life).

220. **Answer: C**

The accounting rate of return is calculated as:

ARR = Annual incremental accounting income/ Initial (or average) investment

By rearranging the formula: Initial investment = Incremental annual income/ARR

Initial investment = [$3,000 − .10 (Initial investment)]/.10

.10 Initial investment = [$3,000 − .10 (Initial investment)]

.20 Initial investment = $3,000

Initial investment = $3,000/.20

Initial investment = $15,000

Proof: $15,000 = [$3,000 − (.10× $15,000)]/.10

$15,000 = [$3,000 − $1,500]/.10

$15,000 = $1,500/.10 = $15,000

221. **Answer: D**

The accounting rate of return measures the expected annual incremental accounting income from a project as a percent of the initial (or average) investment in the project. It considers the entire life of the project and it assumes that the incremental net income is the same each year, including by using an average (Statements I and III, respectively).

222. **Answer: D**

The net investment in working capital would be recognized as a cash outflow of $12,000, and the recovery of the working capital at the end of the project would be recognized at its present value of $6,809. That present value would be computed as $12,000 × PV of $1 for 5 years at 12%, or $12,000 × 0.5674 = $6,809.

223. **Answer: C**

The net present value of the new machine is determined as the present value of future cash inflows less the present value of the current costs of the machine. The facts of this question contain two cash inflows: (1) the cash inflow of $25,000 per year for six years; and (2) the cash inflow from the salvage value of $20,000 at the end of the asset's life. The present values of those inflows are $25,000 × 4.355 (the present value of an annuity for six years) = $108,875 and $20,000 × .564 (the present value of $1 discounted for six years) = $11,280, for a total of $108,875 + $11,280 = $120,155. The present value of the cost of the new machine is $100,000. Thus, the net present value of the machine is $120,155 − $100,000 = $20,155.

224. **Answer: C**

The project with the largest after-tax [net] cash inflow would be project B, with a net cash inflow of $635. The net cash inflow would be computed as: $1,500 − $700 = $800 × (1 − .30) = $800 × .70 = $560 + ($250 × .30) = $560 + $75 = $635. The ($250 × .30) is the tax savings from the deductibility of the depreciation for tax purposes.

225. **Answer: C**

The internal rate of return metric equates the present value of a project's expected cash inflows to the present value of the project's expected costs. It does so by determining the discount (interest) rate that equates the present value of the project's future cash inflows with the present value of the project's cash outflows. The rate so determined is the rate of return earned on the project.

226. **Answer: B**

The internal rate of return on a project is defined as the discount rate at which the net present value of the project equals zero. Specifically, the internal rate of return assesses a project by determining the discount rate that equates the present value of the project's future cash inflows with the present value of the project's future cash outflows.

227. **Answer: C**

The formula used to calculate the profitability index is project net present value divided by the project cost. The resulting percentage gives a ranking that takes into account both project net present value and initial cost. The higher the percentage, the higher the project rank.

228. Answer: D

Because the profitability index is based on cash flow and because projects may be of very long duration, the use of the profitability index requires detailed long-term forecasts (i.e., amount and timing) of projects' cash flows. The longer the projection period, the greater the uncertainty of those cash flows.

229. Answer: A

Project X has a profitability index of 1.50, computed as NPV = $60,000/Cost = $40,000. Project Y has a profitability index of 1.25 and Project Z has an index of .60. Therefore, Project X, with the highest profitability index, would be the most desirable project.

230. Answer: D

The minimum return (rate) used when applying the net present value approach should be equal to or greater than the firm's weighted-average cost of capital. This amount is computed as:

Long-term debt	60%	×	7.1% =	4.26%
Preferred stock	20%	×	10.5% =	2.10%
Common stock	20%	×	14.2% =	2.84%
				9.20%

231. Answer: C

The company will undertake Project C because it has the highest NPV. Specifically, the NPV of Project C is $1,830,000 expected cash inflows − $1,400,000 expected cash outflows = $430,000 NPV, which is greater than the NPV of the other projects.

232. Answer: D

The profitability index (PI) method of capital project evaluation should be the method used in comparing capital projects when capital rationing needs to be considered. The profitability index method (also called the cost/benefit ratio) is primarily intended for use in ranking projects. It does so by taking into account both the present value and the cost of each project.

233. Answer: A

Financial Structure includes all items of liabilities and owners' equity, and capital structure includes long-term liabilities and owners' equity. Since bonds payable, which mature in 10 years, are a long-term liability, they are included in both financial and capital structure of a firm.

234. Answer: C

Financial structure includes all debt and all owners' equity.

235. Answer: A

Short-term debt likely would not be considered when computing the weighted average cost of capital. Short-term debt is not considered part of the capital structure of an entity.

236. Answer: C

Short-term financing is normally concerned with financing for one year or less.

237. Answer: A

Both pledging of accounts receivable and factoring accounts receivable are considered means of short-term financing. In pledging of accounts receivable, the receivables are used as collateral in a financing agreement with a lender. In factoring of accounts receivable, the receivables are sold at a discount for cash to a factor.

238. Answer: C

The annual interest rate of forgoing the cash discount is calculated as:

[Discount %/(1.00 − Discount %)]
   × [360/(40 − 10)]

For the facts given, the calculation would be:

[.02/(1.00 − .02)] × [360/30]
= .02041 × 12 = .2449 (or 24.49%)

239. Answer: D

As a form of short-term financing, short-term notes usually provide cash which often may be used for various asset and expense purposes.

240. Answer: C

The effective rate of interest on the loan is 6.7% and is computed as the net proceeds from the loan divided into the cost of the loan. The cost of the loan is $1,200 ($20,000 × .06 = $1,200) and the net proceeds is $18,000 ($20,000 − [.10 × $20,000] = $18,000); the remaining $2,000 must be maintained as a compensating balance. Thus, the effective interest is: $1,200/$18,000 = 6.666%.

241. Answer: B

A revolving credit agreement is a formal legal commitment, usually by a bank, to extend credit up to some maximum amount to a borrower over a stated period.

242. **Answer: B**

A letter of credit would be used to assure a foreign supplier of payment. A letter of credit is a conditional commitment to pay a third party in accordance with specified terms.

243. **Answer: B**

Under a floating lien agreement the borrower gives the lender a lien against its inventory, but retains control of the inventory and can continuously sell and replace the inventory.

244. **Answer: C**

In a field warehouse agreement, the inventory that serves as security for a borrowing remains with the borrower, but is place under the control of an independent third party. (Also, in a terminal warehouse agreement, the inventory is moved to a public warehouse and placed under the control of an independent third party.)

245. **Answer: C**

The amount held in reserve was .10 × $200,000, or $20,000. During the 30-day period of the factor agreement, $10,000 of the accounts receivable factored had to be reversed because of sales returns and allowances. Therefore, at the end of the 30-day period, Factorco would pay Nexco the remaining $10,000 ($20,000 reserve − $10,000 reversed = $10,000).

246. **Answer: C**

The weighted average cost of capital for a firm is determined by the cost of its long-term financing, not by its short-term financing.

247. **Answer: A**

Long-term financing is comprised of elements that make up capital structure; that is, long-term debt and equity. Financial structure is comprised of both short-term and long-term sources of financing and hence includes capital structure. Therefore, components of long-term financing are part (elements) of both capital structure and financial structure.

248. **Answer: C**

The use of trade accounts payable (a current liability) is a means of short-term financing, not long-term financing.

249. **Answer: C**

Leasing is the better alternative by $1,870, correctly computed as follows:

Purchase Alternative		
Description of Cash Flows	PV factor	PV of Cash Flows
Purchase price = $18,000	1.000	−$18,000 (Outflow)
Tax shield = $3,000/yr × .25 tax rate = $750/yr	3.993	+ 2,995 (Savings)
Maintenance cost = $500/yr	3.993	−1,997 (Outflow)
Opportunity cost of savings		
$18,000 × .02 = $360/yr	3.993	−1,437 (Lost income)
Present Value of Purchasing Alternative		−$18,439 (Net outflow)

Leasing Alternative		
Description of Cash Flows	PV factor	PV of Cash Flows
Lease payments = $5,000/yr	4.312	−$21,560 (Outflow)
Tax shield = $5,000/yr × .25 tax rate = $1,250	3.993	+ 4,991 (Savings)
Present Value of Leasing Alternative		−$16,569 (Net outflow)

Difference between Alternatives—Excess Cost of Purchasing over Leasing $1,870

250. **Answer: A**

Under a net lease, the lessee assumes the executory costs associated with the asset during the lease, including such elements as maintenance, taxes and insurance. In a net-net lease, the lessee assumes responsibility for the executory costs during the life of the lease, as well as for a residual value at the end of the lease.

251. **Answer: D**

The primary reason for a company to agree to a debt covenant limiting the percentage of its long-term debt would be to reduce the risk, and therefore the interest rate, on debt being issued. Debt covenants place contractual limitations on activities of the borrower to help protect the lender. As such, they reduce the default risk associated with a debt issue and, therefore, reduce the interest rate on that debt.

252. **Answer: D**

The primary reason a company would agree to a debt covenant limiting the percentage of its long-term debt would be to reduce the interest rate on the bonds being sold. A debt covenant limiting the percentage of its long-term debt would give the bondholders greater certainty of repayment and, thus, reduce the risk associated with the new bond issue. The reduced risk would lower the interest rate demanded by investors.

253. **Answer: B**

Eurobonds are issued in a currency other than the currency of the country in which they are issued. For example, U.S dollar-denominated bonds issued in an EEU country would be Eurobonds. Because they are not issued in the country of the currency in which they are denominated, these bonds are not subject to the government regulations of the country of the currency and, thus, avoid expense and disclosure requirements of that country.

254. **Answer: C**

Debenture bonds are unsecured bonds. Because they are unsecured, they are likely to have a higher coupon rate (interest rate) than comparable secured bonds.

255. **Answer: B**

Floating-rate bonds are most likely to maintain a constant market value. The rate of interest paid on floating-rate bonds (also called variable-rate bonds/debt) varies with the changes in some underlying benchmark, usually a market interest rate benchmark (e.g., LIBOR or the Fed Funds Rate). Because the interest rate changes with changes in the market rate of interest, they maintain a relatively stable (constant) market value.

256. **Answer: C**

The expected rate of return on the preferred stock (P/S) is determined as the annual dividend on the stock divided by the market price of the stock. This correct answer is computed as: Annual Dividend on P/S $6.40 / Market Price of P/S $80 = .08 (or 8%).

257. **Answer: D**

Preferred stock and common stock are most likely to be different in terms of voting rights; preferred stock typically does not have voting rights and virtually all common stock does.

258. **Answer: B**

Since dividends on preferred stock are not tax deductible, no adjustment to the pre-tax cost needs to be made. Therefore, the after-tax cost of preferred stock is the same as the pre-tax cost, 12%.

259. **Answer: C**

Crowdfunding must take place through a SEC-registered broker-dealer or funding portal (Statement I) and an investor is limited in the amount that can be invested through crowdfunding during a 12-month period to $100,000 (Statement III).

260. **Answer: D**

The dollar return on stock consists of both the dividends received ($5) and the change in stock price ($10). The rate of return on stock is calculated as the dollar return divided by the dollar amount of the investment on which the return was earned. Thus, the correct calculation is: ($5 + $10) / $50 = $15 / $50 = 30%.

261. **Answer: B**

Issuing common stock to finance its projects would best meet Bander's financing strategy. Specifically, issuing common stock would (1) not result in fixed charges, since dividends are at the discretion of the Board of Directors, (2) not result in a fixed maturity date, since common stock does not mature, and (3) would likely increase the credit-worthiness of the company because the issuance of additional common stock would reduce its debt to equity ratio by increasing equity.

262. **Answer: C**

The cost of new (marginal) equity is 16%, which would include the cost associated with flotation of the new issue. The after-tax cost of new debt would be the before-tax cost of 9% less the tax savings resulting from the deductibility of interest on the debt, which would be computed as 9% × (1.00 − .50) = .09 × .50 = .045 (or 4.5%).

263. **Answer: D**

The cost of debt most frequently is measured as the actual interest rate minus the tax savings. The tax savings result because the interest expense is deductible for tax purposes and the resulting tax savings reduce the effective cost (and rate) of debt financing. For example, if the stated (actual) interest rate is 10% and the tax rate is 40%, the effective interest rate (actual interest rate minus tax savings) will be $10\% \times (1.00 - .40)$, or $10\% \times .60 = 6\%$ effective cost of debt.

264. **Answer: A**

Other things being equal, the higher the tax rate of a firm, the greater the benefit from debt financing because the cost of debt (interest expense) is tax deductible and therefore generates a tax savings. That tax savings offsets the nominal cost of the debt. Since interest is not paid on dividends to equity holders and since dividends are not tax deductible, there is no comparable savings related to equity financing.

265. **Answer: C**

Reducing investment in current assets is likely to increase the risk that inventory shortages will increase. Excessive reductions in inventory may result in inventory shortages, which cause interruptions in operations and an inability to meet production requirements.

266. **Answer: A**

A firm can either over invest or under invest in net working capital. If it over invests it has cash or inventory that exceed immediate needs or its accounts receivable are excessive. Those (net) assets are not being used effectively and, therefore, are not providing the return that could otherwise be earned. If a firm under invests, it has inadequate cash or inventory to meet immediate needs.

267. **Answer: D**

Property, plant, and equipment is not an element of working capital. Although management of property, plant, and equipment would be a management concern, it would not be a factor in the management of working capital, which is comprised of current assets and current liabilities.

268. **Answer: D**

The gross annual benefit from the lock-box arrangement would be the $100,000 collected per day times 2 days reduced collection time multiplied by the interest received on the accelerated collections. That calculation is: ($100,000× 2) × .06 = $200,000 × .06 = $12,000 savings. The gross annual cost of the lock-box arrangement is the $500 per month multiplied by 12 months. The net annual benefit is $12,000 savings – $6,000 cost = $6,000 net benefit.

269. **Answer: A**

The general objective of cash management is to maintain a cash balance between holding too little cash and holding too much cash.

A firm must maintain adequate cash on an on-going basis to meet its cash-requiring obligations that arise in the normal course of its business activities—accounts payable, salaries and wages, etc.

On the other hand, holding too much cash (excess cash over that needed for immediate obligations) is an inefficient use of resources, since the return on unneeded cash usually is less than could be earned if the cash were invested in assets with a higher return (e.g., securities, inventory, capital projects, etc.).

270. **Answer: B**

A zero-balance account is a cash management technique that permits control over cash outflows by using a checking account that has a zero ($0) real balance because payments made from the account exactly equal deposits to the account. From a financial management perspective, a zero-balance account arrangement enables decentralized units to write checks drawn on one of that unit's accounts that has no real balance.

As those checks clear the bank they create a temporary negative balance in the account. At the end of each day, the bank transfers an amount from another of the firm's accounts to exactly cover the negative balance in the account. Thus, it is a zero-balance account.

Zero-balance accounts also are used in another way to control cash disbursements, often as an element of internal control. In this context, a firm deposits to an account only an amount equal to known payments to be made from that account. For example, a firm might use a zero-balance account for its payroll. Once the dollar amount of the payroll checks is determined, only that amount is deposited to the account against which the checks are drawn. As a consequence, no more than the total amount of payroll checks can be paid out of the account. In addition, it is easier to reconcile the account and the real balance will be zero.

271. **Answer: A**

In selecting short-term investments for "excess" cash, a firm would be concerned with (1) safety of principal, (2) price stability of the investment instrument, and (3) ability to readily convert the investment to cash without undue cost.

272. **Answer: D**

The risk associated with the ability to sell an investment in a short period of time without having to make significant price concessions is liquidity risk. Two possible elements are implied in the risk: (1) the inability to sell for cash in the short term, and (2) the inability to receive fair value in cash in the short term.

273. **Answer: D**

Treasury Bills are debt obligation of the U.S. government, have a maturity of one year or less, and are backed by the full faith and credit of the U.S. government. Treasury Bills are considered the safest securities available to the U.S. investor.

274. **Answer: B**

The March 31 balance in accounts receivable consists only of 25% of March credit sales. Since all sales are collected by the end of the month following the sales, only 25% of March sales would remain outstanding as of March 31. The amount is calculated as .25 × $50,000 = $12,500.

275. **Answer: D**

Asher likely lengthened its discount period to meet terms offered by competitors (Statement II), and to seek to stimulate sales (Statement III). It would not have lengthened its discount period to increase the average age of its account receivable (Statement I), but that was an undesirable, but necessary, outcome.

276. **Answer: A**

The benefits obtained would be the reduction in working capital required for carrying average accounts receivable of $30,000 multiplied by

the opportunity cost of .15 = $4,500. The cost of the plan would be the reduced cash collected on accounts receivable of .02 times the 40% expected to take advantage of the discount (.02 × .40 = .008) times the credit sales, or .008 × $1,000,000 = $8,000. So, the net results would be an increase in cost of $4,500 − $8,000 = − $3,500. Although not clearly stated in the problem "facts," the decrease is intended to be average accounts receivable. As this is an actual AICPA exam question, the wording has been left unchanged.

277. **Answer: B**

Determining the level of stock (inventory) at which the inventory should be reordered is a function of the minimum level of inventory to be maintained, referred to as the safety stock, and the length of time it takes to receive inventory after it is ordered, referred to as the lead-time or delivery-time stock. Both the safety stock and the lead-time stock are based on the rate of inventory usage. The calculation of the reorder point would be: Reorder point = Safety stock + Delivery-time stock. The cost of inventory does not enter into the determination of the reorder point (but it does enter into the optimum quantity to reorder).

278. **Answer: D**

A change in safety stock does not affect a firm's economic order quantity (but does affect its reorder point). The calculation of economic order quantity (EOQ) is:

$$EOQ = \sqrt{\frac{2 \times \text{Annual demand} \times \text{Cost per order}}{\text{Carrying cost per unit}}}$$

Thus, the safety stock is not a factor in determining the economic order quantity, and a change (decrease) in safety stock would have no effect on Dee's economic order quantity.

279. **Answer: A**

The economic order quantity model seeks to determine the order size that will minimize total inventory cost, both order cost and carrying costs.

While the question can be answered quite easily, because the economic order quantity Answer choice A is the only one that is concerned with minimizing total inventory cost by considering carrying cost and restocking cost (reordering costs), the wording of the question is ambiguous at best. It would have been better worded as "Which of the following inventory management approaches seeks to minimize total inventory costs by considering both the restocking (reordering) cost and the carrying costs?" Because it is an actual AICPA exam question, the wording has been left unchanged.

280. **Answer: B**

This option would be the most attractive for Ruby. By borrowing from the bank, paying in 15 days and taking the 1.5% discount would be the most beneficial option. The cost of this option would be computed as:

Discount percentage/(100% − Discount %) × 360 days/(Total pay period − Discount period)

For this option the values would be:

[.015/(1.00 − .015)] × [360/(30 − 15)] = .01522 × 24 = .3653 (or 36.53%), the annual cost of not taking the discount offered. By borrowing from the bank at 10% and taking advantage of the discount, Ruby would benefit by .3653 annual rate saved less .10 annual cost of borrowing = .2653.

281. **Answer: C**

Under the hedging principle of financing, short-term liabilities (e.g., accounts payable or short-term note payable) should be used to finance short-term assets, which would include inventory.

282. **Answer: B**

Under the hedging principle of finance, assets are acquired with financing that matches the life of the asset. Thus, short-term assets would be financed with short-term liabilities and long-term assets would be financed with long-term liabilities or equity. The financing of long-term needs with short-term funds would be an aggressive approach to financing long-term needs that would not be consistent with the hedging principle.

283. **Answer: A**

Ratio analysis and related measures can be used to compare the performance and position of a firm over time and to compare the performance and position of multiple firms.

284. **Answer: D**

Ratio analysis uses monetary measures as well as other quantitative measures. For example,

in the earnings per share calculation, the number of shares of common stock, a non-monetary measure, is used. Ratio analysis also uses financial statement measures in addition to measures that are not a part of financial statements. For example, the price-earnings ratio uses the market price of the stock, a measure not found in the financial statements.

285. **Answer: C**

Price indexes convert prices of one period to what those prices would have been in terms of prices of a prior period. They are not a major purpose or type of measure used in working capital management. Common examples of price indexes are the consumer price index (CPI) and the producer price index (PPI).

286. **Answer: C**

As the name implies, fixed cost to total cost measures the ratio of fixed cost to total cost and is one measure of operating leverage. A high ratio of fixed cost to total cost indicates instability in earnings that results because fixed costs are incurred regardless of the level of revenues. Thus, when fixed costs constitute a high proportion of a firm's total costs, a significant reduction in revenues may result in losses, since the fixed cost will be incurred even in the face of a significant reduction in revenues. Such losses could put the firm at risk for failure.

287. **Answer: D**

The company's times-interest-earned ratio is 10.0. The times-interest-earned ratio measures the ability of current earnings to cover interest payments for a period. It is measured as:

Times-Interest-Earned Ratio = (Net Income + Interest Expense + Income Tax Expense) / Interest Expense

Therefore:

Times-Interest-Earned Ratio	= ($5.4M + $1M + $3.6M*)/ $1M
	= $10M/$1M = 10.0 times

Income before taxes is computed as: .6X = $5.4M (i.e., 60% of taxable income equals $5.4M). Therefore: X (income before taxes) = $5.4M/.6 = $9.0M. Income before taxes = $9.0M − income after taxes = $5.4M = income taxes = $3.6M.)

The $10M also can be determined as $9.0 income before taxes + $1M interest expense = $10M.

288. **Answer: C**

The quick (or acid-test) ratio is .750. The quick ratio measures the quantitative relationship between highly liquid assets and current liabilities in terms of the "number of times" that cash and assets that can be converted quickly to cash cover current liabilities. It is computed as:

Acid-test Ratio = (Cash + (Net) Receivables + Marketable Securities) / Current Liabilities

For the facts given, the calculation is:

$5,000 + $10,000/$15,000 + $5,000, or

$15,000/$20,000 = .750 quick (acid-test) ratio

Inventory is not considered an asset that can be quickly converted to cash; long-term note payable is not a current liability.

289. **Answer: B**

The number of days' sales outstanding measures the average number of days required to collect receivables. A reduction in the number of days' sales outstanding would serve increase cash by collecting cash sooner and reducing the amount of accounts receivable outstanding.

290. **Answer: C**

The cash cycle can be determined as the operating cycle (i.e., inventory conversion cycle [24 days] + accounts receivable conversion cycle [18 days]) less the accounts payable conversion cycle [21 days]. Thus, Cyco's cash cycle would be computed as 24 + 18 = 42 − 21 = 21 days, the correct answer.

291. **Answer: B**

Inventory turnover is computed as: Cost of Goods Sold/Average Inventory. Cost of goods sold (COGS) is the sum of beginning inventory (BI) plus purchases (P), which equals cost of goods available for sale (COGAS), less ending inventory (EI); that difference is cost of goods sold. It would be computed as: BI $17,000 + P $56,000 = COGAS $73,000 − (EI) $13,000 = (COGS) $60,000. Average inventory (AI) is computed as (BI) $17,000 + (EI) $13,000/2, or (AI) $30,000/2 = $15,000. Thus, inventory turnover is (COGS) $60,000/(AI) $15,000 = 4.

292. **Answer: B**

The cash conversion cycle measures the time between when cash is paid to suppliers and when cash is collected from customers. It is computed using the inventory conversion cycle (DIO) plus the accounts receivable conversion cycle (DPO) less the accounts payable conversion cycle (DPO). For this question, the computation is:

293. **Answer: C**

Risks that can be reduced by diversification (also called diversifiable risk or unsystematic risk) are risks that relate to a particular undertaking, firm or industry, and typically are not associated with macroeconomic conditions. Diversifiable risk are mitigated by engaging in multiple different investments or undertakings so that an unexpected unfavorable outcome of one investment or undertaking will represent only a small portion of all investments or undertakings and so that unfavorable outcomes on some investments or undertakings will be offset by favorable outcomes on other investments or undertakings. Labor strikes typically are peculiar to a particular undertaking, plant, firm or industry and are, therefore, diversifiable by having labor forces in other undertakings, plants, or industries.

294. **Answer: D**

A swap agreement would be recommended to hedge interest rate risk on long-term floating-rate bonds. In an interest rate swap agreement one stream of future interest payments (e.g., floating-rate payments) is exchanged for another stream of future interest payments (e.g., fixed-rate payments) for a specified principal amount. In this case, an interest rate swap would hedge (mitigate) exposure to fluctuations in interest rates of the floating-rate bonds by exchanging those payments for a fixed-rate payment.

295. **Answer: A**

Of the alternative Answer Choices listed, during a period of high inflation, the best investment is precious metals. Because of their scarcity, precious metals tend to increase in market value during periods of inflation. Treasury bonds and corporate bonds, both of which typically pay fixed rates of return, face market interest rate risk and will lose market value as inflation drives up the general rate of interest. While common stock may provide some protection during a period of high inflation, that inflation causes the costs of productive inputs to increase, therefore, increasing pressure on company profits and returns to common stock shareholders.

296. **Answer: A**

Both receivables and payables (and investments or other accounts) denominated (to be settled) in a foreign currency are subject to currency exchange risk. That risk derives from changes in the rate of exchange between currencies, which could either increase or decrease and cause the dollar value of an item to decrease.

297. **Answer: A**

It is common for computerized systems to combine functions that would be considered incompatible in a manual system (for example, in computerized systems, a single employee is often responsible for creating the deposit and posting the transactions to the cash receipts journal, the accounts receivable sub ledger, and the general ledger).

This can occur because the system limits the transactions that it is possible for the employee to record, creating a compensating control.

298. **Answer: D**

This is the best answer since engaging the owner in the activities of the business is an important compensating control in small organizations.

299. **Answer: C**

Statement II is correct. Automated transaction processing results in a greater uniformity of transactions.

300. **Answer: A**

This task is not a part of assessing how IT can best contribute to business objectives.

301. **Answer: A**

The purpose of IT governance is to strategically manage and acquire IT resources in support of the organization's mission. This requires balancing the risks and returns from IT assets.

302. **Answer: C**

The process of reviewing system response logs is within the "monitor the processes" (M1) activity, which falls within the "monitor and evaluate" domain. Therefore, this is the correct answer.

303. **Answer: D**

ERPs provide transaction processing, management support, and decision-making support in a single, integrated package. By integrating all data and processes of an organization into a unified system, ERPs attempt to eliminate many of the problems faced by organizations when they attempt to consolidate information from operations in multiple departments, regions, or divisions. This is the correct answer since facilitating information exchange and collaboration is the primary purpose of the proposed system.

304. **Answer: C**

SaaS is the use of the cloud to access software.

305. **Answer: B**

PaaS is the use of the cloud to create (not access) software.

306. **Answer: C**

If she changes both live and archive copies of programs, changes that she has made may not be detected.

307. **Answer: C**

Failing to remove user accounts upon termination of employees is an important control risk, and it is directly relevant to the case facts.

308. **Answer: C**

The separation of the data entry function from the application programming function is critical to the segregation of duties within an IT department. This is because if one both enters data and changes the programs into which those data are entered, one can perpetrate consequential financial frauds. This is why data entry occurs within the operations unit of an IT department and application development occurs within the development function of an IT department. These functions must be kept separate and their duties segregated. Therefore, this is the best answer to the question.

309. **Answer: B**

This is an example of a product differentiation strategy since competitors are unlikely to be able to sell this same product.

310. **Answer: C**

This statement is true. Therefore, this is the correct answer since selling a digitized product can reduce costs and improve quality (e.g., some online books are cheaper, include hyperlinks to resources and key terms, and include additional content).

311. **Answer: C**

This is a data-drive DSS that is engaging in data mining.

312. **Answer: D**

ESS are most likely to include external data.

313. **Answer: C**

This is a data-drive DSS that is engaging in data mining.

314. **Answer: B**

A data mart is focused on a particular market or purpose and contains only information specific to that objective.

315. **Answer: C**

A data mart is more specialized than a data warehouse. The data mart is often constructed to support specific needs of subunits of an organization.

316. **Answer: D**

Statement one is incorrect because, while flat file systems do contain program independence, this is seen as a disadvantage not an advantage. This is because the program independence of flat file systems means that multiple programs must be used to read, access and process the data. Statement II is incorrect because flat file systems contain a high degree of data redundancy.

317. **Answer: D**

Database management software is considered both software and middleware.

318. **Answer: D**

A, B, and C are all categories of computer software. Because of this, the correct answer is D—all of the above.

319. **Answer: C**

This answer lists the data structures in the correct order. Specifically, a character has fewer pieces of data than does a field. A field has fewer pieces of data than does a record. And a record has fewer pieces of data than does a file.

320. **Answer: D**

Solid state drive (SSD) storage has the desired characteristics.

321. **Answer: C**

CD-ROM is the best choice of the available answers. It can handle a large volume of data and is suited to data that changes infrequently.

322. **Answer: D**

This answer is incorrect. Given the decades of refinement of them, mainframes are generally more reliable than microcomputers.

323. **Answer: A**

Speed! It's all about speed here. Loan applicants want fast answers. They are impatient! Quickly! Run the data quickly! Gimme my money! Now!

324. **Answer: D**

An online, real-time system would be appropriate for airline reservations.

325. **Answer: B**

This answer is consistent with the batch processing system and the detailed posting of transactions.

326. **Answer: D**

This statement is true.

327. **Answer: D**

This statement is true.

328. **Answer: B**

A cycle time in manufacturing is the time required to produce an order. In computer science, it is the time between one random access memory event to the next. Neither of these definitions is relevant to the IoT.

329. **Answer: C**

This is a traditional accounting data source. Therefore, while these data will find their way into a big data pool (eventually), this is the least likely to be an example of big data, from the offered alternatives.

330. **Answer: D**

What do attrition and retention have to do with big data? Why would attrition and retention be higher with big data? Attrition and retention of what, the data or the employees?

331. **Answer: A**

Big data uses existing data warehouses. but data warehousing is not a direct enabler of big data.

332. **Answer: D**

The ledger is implemented in blockchain; the network is peer-to-peer.

333. **Answer: A**

The described characteristics are consistent with the use of a blockchain system.

334. **Answer: B**

If accounting transactions are stored on an automated, secured network, then auditing and compliance costs should go down.

335. **Answer: C**

Intelligent agents interact with humans (e.g., Siri® on the Apple® iPhone®) and have natural language processing ability.

336. **Answer: B**

AI systems require fast computers since they are computing intensive. In addition, most AI systems require the analysis of big data sets to be useful.

337. **Answer: A**

Machine learning is a goal of AI systems, not a risk.

338. **Answer: B**

According to the AICPA ASEC principles, this is the definition of availability.

339. **Answer: B**

According to the AICPA ASEC principles, this is the definition of processing integrity.

340. **Answer: A**

According to the AICPA ASEC principles, security is the foundation of systems reliability.

341. **Answer: B**

This statement is true. This is an example of internally communicating information to support the functioning of internal controls.

342. **Answer: C**

This statement is accurate. The example illustrates external communication (with a consortium of accounting firms) about internal control.

343. **Answer: C**

Managing cyber risks begins with identifying system value and protecting systems according to their value.

344. **Answer: A**

The organization is exploring "how is it doing?" at a high level related to cybersecurity. Hence, the function is "identify" and, because the focus is on high-level objectives, the element is "categories."

345. **Answer: D**

This is an inappropriate application of the framework for cybersecurity, since organizational risk management is a broader process than the risk management process specified in the framework for cybersecurity.

346. **Answer: B**

An external auditor cannot assure a client that control deficiencies will be corrected since the auditor is not a part of correcting the deficiencies. This is an inherent limitation of auditing that is unchanged by the framework for cybersecurity.

347. **Answer: A**

This is a false statement. IT policies need not relate specifically to physical or electronic threats to IT.

348. **Answer: B**

This is a false statement.The description given is of the "service management and operational service problem solving" policy.

349. **Answer: C**

IT policies are particularly important in decentralized companies since IT services are likely to be less under the control of management.

350. **Answer: D**

This is an example of e-procurement, in which a company seeks bids to provide a product or service.

351. Answer: B

Viral marketing is the use of e-commerce or e-business to increase brand awareness or sales.

352. Answer: C

Limited growth is a risk of failing to implement e-commerce, not a risk of e-commerce.

353. Answer: C

Encryption can be used to ensure the privacy and security of EDI messages both during transmission and when stored. Hardware-based encryption is inherently more secure than software-based encryption, as software can be more easily accessed and altered than hardware.

354. Answer: B

Cash cards do not involve bank clearing processes and are not considered to be EFT transactions.

355. Answer: B

This is the best answer Because increased security is a common motivation for the use of a value-added network.

356. Answer: A

The engagement of the owner in a small entity is likely to improve the assessment of risks because of their hands-on involvement with all levels of personnel.

357. Answer: C

Employees are likely to be more engaged and committed to the organization when working from home than when working at the office. In addition, allowing employees to work from home increases the availability of the company's systems to employees.

358. Answer: D

This is not an example of IT outsourcing. An internal, private cloud is not shared and is wholly owned and managed within an entity.

359. Answer: D

All of the above statements are true.

360. Answer: A

Authorization is most likely to be absent in a small business computing environment. There is a great need for third-party review and testing within the small business computing environment.

361. Answer: D

View-only access is a useful control (i.e., restriction) on the ability of mobile devices to make changes in data.

362. Answer: C

A concern for customized systems would suggest the use of a decentralized system.

363. Answer: D

This is the very definition of a hybrid or distributed database system.

364. Answer: C

This question presumes a knowledge of the Grimms' fairy tale, "The Story of the Three Bears." In the fairy tale, Goldilocks wants her porridge neither too hot, nor too cold. Hence, the "Goldilocks" solution, which is sought by this question in relation to computing and file sharing, is a solution that is neither too centralized, nor too decentralized (metaphorically, neither too hot nor too cold).

Hence, this is the correct answer—a compromise between centralized and decentralized computing.

365. Answer: B

Fiber optic cable is a higher-cost, higher-quality choice for a wired network.

366. Answer: B

LANs use dedicated lines, but WANs use public or shared lines. Hence, I is true, but II is not.

367. Answer: D

Bluetooth is designed for exactly this scenario, i.e., short-range, low power communication, for example, between an ear piece and a cell phone.

368. Answer: B

Transmission control protocol/Internet protocol (TCP/IP) is the protocol used by the Internet.

369. Answer: B

XBRL is specifically designed to exchange financial information over the World Wide Web.

370. Answer: B

Gateways connect Internet computers of dissimilar networks.

371. Answer: B

Headers are used to identify data records in an accounting system file.

372. Answer: C

Fire suppression systems in a computer facility should not use halon, because it is an environmental hazard.

373. Answer: C

This answer is correct because an operating system ordinarily requires no physical layout space since it represents software within a computer.

374. Answer: B

With improving technologies, biometrics are likely the strongest method for accessing systems.

375. Answer: B

The goal of biometrics is to authenticate the user.

376. Answer: D

"Application firewalls" are separate and distinct from "network firewalls": the terms definitely do *not* refer to the same program. Network firewalls perform relatively low-level filtering capabilities; application firewalls have the ability to do much more sophisticated checks and provide much better control.

377. Answer: B

In asymmetric encryption, the receiver (Cassie) has the private key.

378. Answer: D

A virtual private network (VPN) is a secure way to create an encrypted communication tunnel to allow remote users secure access to a network. The VPN uses authentication to identify users and encryption to prevent unauthorized users from intercepting data.

379. Answer: D

This answer is correct because encryption involves coding of the data files and, accordingly, encrypted sensitive data provides security because the files cannot be read by those without knowledge of the encryption code.

380. Answer: B

This information would contribute to the development of a disaster recovery plan.

381. Answer: B

Determine business continuity strategies is the third step in BCM but it is the earliest procedure listed for this question.

382. Answer: C

Mission-critical tasks are given first priority in DRP.

383. Answer: C

Checkpoints are mostly used in batch systems. The use of checkpoint and restart is an important backup procedure.

384. Answer: D

A fault tolerant system includes redundant components.

385. Answer: D

Mirroring is a high-cost, high-reliability approach to backup that is common in e-commerce applications. Of the offered alternatives in this question, this is the best approach to assuring the continuous delivery of services despite a natural disaster.

386. Answer: D

From the very simple description of events in this case, this is the best answer.

387. Answer: A

A denial-of-service attack prevents legitimate users from accessing the system by flooding the server with hundreds of incomplete access requests. The object of the attack is to prevent access to the system: the attacker does not actually gain access to information on the system.

388. **Answer: D**

In a denial of service attack, servers are overwhelmed with incomplete access requests, causing them to hang, zombie like, in a living, though brain-dead, useless state.

389. **Answer: B**

Creating system documentation would be an appropriate data-gathering technique for a system survey.

390. **Answer: D**

After changes and verification to those changes, source programs move into production.

391. **Answer: A**

The management of changes to applications is part of the Source Program Library Management System (SPLMS).

392. **Answer: D**

Closed-loop verification helps ensure that a valid and correct customer account has been entered; after the code is entered, this system looks up and displays additional information about the selected code. For example, the operator enters a customer code, and the system displays the customer's name and address.

393. **Answer: D**

April has only 30 days. The reasonableness test will catch this error.

394. **Answer: A**

This answer is correct because a record count is simply a count of the number of records in a batch.

395. **Answer: D**

A parity check is designed to detect errors in data transmission.

396. **Answer: D**

Password strength is increased when passwords are longer, when they include numbers, letters, and special characters, and when both uppercase and lowercase letters are included.

Although this password does not include special characters, it does contain numerals,

uppercase letters and lowercase letters and is, therefore, the strongest password listed.

397. **Answer: C**

The distribution of reports is considered an output control.

398. **Answer: A**

The accounting cycle as a sequence of steps begins by recording business transactions.

399. **Answer: B**

Journal entries are first recorded in general journals. Then they are posted to ledger accounts.

400. **Answer: D**

Money (or credit) from the financing cycle is used to buy raw materials in the expenditure cycle, which is then sent to the production cycle.

401. **Answer: B**

A sales (or customer) invoice documents a sale and the billing of the customer for the sale.

402. **Answer: C**

A picking ticket identifies the items to be pulled for a sales order.

403. **Answer: B**

Allowing the credit manager to set the credit limit is most likely to result in following organizational policy related to the setting of customer credit limits.

404. **Answer: A**

A purchase order formally requests a supplier to sell and deliver specified products at designated prices. Better controls over this document would most likely have caught this violation of policy.

405. **Answer: A**

Segregation of the receiving function from the purchasing function would help prevent the violation because, if all purchase orders had to be checked in by a separate receiving department, we would detect the mis-delivered order.

406. **Answer: D**

An automated receiving system that includes multiple scans of received goods is likely to have caught this error.

407. **Answer: B**

A materials requisition, also called a "materials transfer ticket," would authorize Hamish to move the sprocket from raw materials to production.

408. **Answer: A**

The bill of materials specifies which parts are used in making a product. This is what Hamish needs.

409. **Answer: D**

A master production schedule will be helpful in reducing excess production of inventory.

410. **Answer: B**

Direct deposits move directly to employees' accounts, thereby lessening the likelihood that checks are deposited by someone other than employees.

411. **Answer: C**

This report would be helpful in matching employee skills (from the report) to the new job duty.

412. **Answer: D**

This is the function that should have determined whether the hired workers could legally be employed.

413. **Answer: B**

Because credit sales should appear in the subsidiary ledger (and obviously, in aggregate, in the control account), this activity will be useful in determining that all credit sales are recorded.

414. **Answer: C**

This is the purpose of closing journal entries.

415. **Answer: D**

Unusual, manually posted entries are of greater concern because they may indicate fraud or earnings management.

416. **Answer: B**

The case describes this as a "preliminary" system design. This is a part of conceptual systems design.

417. **Answer: B**

Direct cutover would be the riskiest, since all locations would implement simultaneously.

418. **Answer: B**

Also called the plunge or big bang approach. The old system is dropped and the new system is put in place all at once.

419. **Answer: A**

An internal failure cost is incurred when a product that does not conform to its design specifications is detected before shipment to customers. The cost to rework items that do not meet design specifications is incurred before the items are shipped, and therefore, qualify as internal failure costs. Other internal failure costs include spoilage, scrap, and breakdown maintenance.

Responding to customer complaints occurs after items are shipped, and therefore, is not included in internal failure costs. The cost of receiving and responding to customer complaints is a component of external failure costs.

Statistical quality control programs are designed to distinguish between in-control and out-of-control operations, and thus, to signal when to investigate the operation, determine the problem, and solve the problem. These programs are partially preventive in nature because they often provide signals of developing problems that have not yet reached the point where remedial action is cost-effective. These programs also play an appraisal role in identifying units that fail to conform to design specifications. Their cost is incurred regardless of whether the product fails to meet its design specifications.

420. **Answer: C**

One of the striking effects of a JIT system is the lowered level of inventory maintained by the firm. Rather than maintain a large amount of inventory as a buffer for stockouts, the JIT system purchases inventory only when necessary. The inventory is to arrive just in time for its use in production or sales. Thus, much less inventory must be maintained at any one time.

Inventory turnover = cost of goods sold/ average inventory. Inventory percentage = ending inventory balance/total assets. With lower amounts of inventory on hand at any time, inventory turnover INCREASES because its denominator decreases, and inventory percentage DECREASES because its numerator decreases by a greater percentage than does its denominator. Inventories turnover much more frequently because the quantity on hand is so small and inventory is sold soon after it is acquired or produced.

421. **Answer: B**

Six Sigma is the only well-recognized quality program used to minimize defects while reducing costs.

422. **Answer: B**

The customer perspective evaluates the organization's success in targeted customer and market segments.

423. **Answer: C**

Benchmarking provides a relevant comparison when trying to achieve the optimal outcome by comparing to others.

424. **Answer: D**

All three measures are relevant to the evaluation of how a manufacturing system is performing. Throughput time is the total time required for an item to make its way through the manufacturing system. The ratio of setup time to total production time reflects the adaptability of the system to required changes in production capability. If this ratio is excessive, the firm is unable to alter its product to meet changing customer demand. The ratio of rework to total units is a measure of quality. A lower ratio indicates higher quality and less interruption to the production process.

425. **Answer: C**

The balanced scorecard is defined somewhat by its four categories of financial, customers, internal business processes, and learning and growth.

426. **Answer: D**

To solve for residual income (RI), you must first solve for assets (investment) and income. Since an asset turnover of 1.5 is sales/investment and sales is $750,000, we use $750,000 / x = 1.5, where x = investment. Thus, investment is $500,000. Since a return on sales of 8% is profit/sales and sales is $750,000, we use x / $750,000 = 8%, where x = income. Thus, income is $60,000. Now, RI = income less the rate given at 12% multiplied by the investment. Thus, RI is 0 = $60,000 − .12 ($500,000).

427. **Answer: C**

The calculation of the weighted average cost of capital (WACC) involves proportional weighting for debt and equity with the debt figure reduced for deductible taxes. Thus, the cost of debt is 1.8% = 50% (6%) (1 − .4); the cost of owners' equity is split for the preferred 0.7% = 10% (7%); and the common 4.6% = 40% (11.5%). Thus, the WACC is 7.1% = 1.8% + 0.7% + 4.6%.

428. **Answer: B**

Cost of debt is equal to 8%, and the debt ratio = debt/equity (40%). stock is to be issued at 10% and debt is weighted at 40% while stock is 60%. Therefore, cost of debt is 8% (.40) = 3.2%; equity is 10% (.60) = 6.0% and 3.2% + 6% = 9.2%.

429. **Answer: B**

Return on investment (ROI) is computed as:

Net income (before interest expense)/ Average total assets

In this question, the amount of interest expense is not given separately. Therefore, the Net income calculation must be based on Sales ($1,150,000) − Operating expenses ($550,000), or $600,000. The average operating assets for the year is computed as: Beginning $5,400,000 + Ending $6,600,000 = $12,000,000/2 = $6,000,000. Thus, the correct calculation is: $600,000/$6,000,000 = .10 (10%).

430. **Answer: D**

Inventory turnover is calculated by dividing the cost of goods sold by the average inventory. Cost of goods sold = $2,525,000(1 − .4) = $1,515,000; average inventory is [.15(2,125,000)

+ .22(2,525,000)] / 2 = $437,125. Thus, inventory turnover = $1,515,000 / $437,125.

431. **Answer: B**

ROI = (income / sales) * asset turnover; and ROI = 25% = $5M / sales * 2.5. Thus, solving for sales, the result is $50M.

432. **Answer: B**

Avoiding costs provides a direct and immediate effect on profits, while increasing revenue often results in at least some proportional cost increases as well.

433. **Answer: A**

Insurance is specifically designed to reduce or eliminate peril or hazard risk where a specific type of risk of loss is involved (i.e., pure risk).

434. **Answer: B**

Hedging offsets exposure to future price fluctuations by locking in a given price in the future. Thus, foreign currency exchange or commodities would provide examples where hedging would be an appropriate risk management technique.

435. **Answer: B**

Systematic risk is also known as market risk or nondiversifiable risk and is associated with large-scale economic events or natural disasters and typically affects all companies to some degree.

436. **Answer: C**

Lean manufacturing is accurately described as using small batches of a high variety of unique products with highly skilled, cross-trained labor.

437. **Answer: A**

The objective of the demand flow or demand flow technology (DFT) approach is to link process flows and manage those flows based on customer demand.

438. **Answer: B**

Six Sigma is very similar to total quality management (TQM) and uses TQM tools such as control charts, run charts, pareto histograms, and Isikawa (fish-bone) diagrams.

439. **Answer: C**

Variable costs are presumed to be avoidable and fixed costs are presumed to be unavoidable to start with. Then $5,000 for rent was avoidable when they decided to buy. Thus, the cost to buy is $95,000 = $80,000 + $15,000 in fixed cost that are presumed unavoidable versus a cost to make of $90,000.

440. **Answer: D**

Journal entries to record the manufacturing cost are similar for job-order and process costing. When overhead is applied, it is debited to work in process. The credit is to factory overhead applied. Work in process receives only applied overhead, unless some underapplied factory overhead is allocated to work in process at the end of the period.

441. **Answer: C**

The issuance (use in production) of indirect materials results in a debit (increase) to factory overhead control. This account accumulates actual overhead cost incurrence. Actual overhead is not debited to work in process. Rather, work in process is debited to factory overhead applied.

442. **Answer: C**

Scrap is the material left over after making a product. It has minimal or no sales value. Scrap is automatically included in work in process for a product because it is part of the material cost of a product. In many manufacturing settings, it is impossible to use every bit of material input. For example, the circular punch-outs for conduit boxes are scrap.

Normal spoilage is output that cannot be sold through normal channels. It is an inherent result of production. In many cases, it is not cost effective to attempt to reduce the normal spoilage cost to zero. It is a normal part of the production process and, therefore, its cost is included in the cost of units produced.

Abnormal spoilage is considered avoidable. It occurs as a result of an unexpected event, such as a machine breakdown or accident. This cost is treated as a loss rather than a normal production cost.

443. **Answer: B**

Normal spoilage is a manufacturing cost because it is an expected and inherent part of production. Thus, it is included in the cost of finished goods. Abnormal spoilage is the amount of spoilage in excess of normal spoilage, and it is treated as a period cost.

The total units completed are 5,500 (5,000 + 200 + 300). Of this total, 5,200 are included in finished goods. Thus, 5,200/5,500 of the total cost incurred is included in finished goods. The remainder is a period cost.

Debit to finished goods = $93,600 = (5,200/5,500)$99,000

444. **Answer: D**

The distinction between normal and abnormal spoilage is that normal spoilage is an expected part of the production process. The cost represents units or materials that were lost in the normal production process. They are indirect manufacturing costs (overhead) and, thus, are inventoriable. Abnormal spoilage is unexpected, and is over and above the anticipated level. It represents a loss for financial accounting purposes. No benefit is derived from abnormal spoilage.

445. **Answer: A**

The key to answering this question is to determine the beginning and ending amounts of raw materials and of finished goods and the differences between the two. These amounts come from beginning FG (multiplied by 5 for FG) and beginning RM amounts as reported between the periods: beginning FG + beginning RM × 5 (40,000 + 50,000) and the same for ending FG + ending RM × 5 (45,000 + 42,000). The sums add up to be 90,000 and 87,000, showing a positive difference of 3,000. Since the company started with 500,000 feet and it has an additional 3,000 feet, it only needs to purchase 497,000 feet to have enough raw materials.

446. **Answer: B**

Given that the truck costs $16,250 per year = 125,000 miles @ $0.13 per mile, and given that the truck has a capacity of 7,000,000 lbs. per year = 250 loads @ 28,000 lbs. each, the cost per lb. is $.00232 = $16,250 / 7,000,000 lbs.

447. **Answer: C**

The following equation must be estimated: y = a + bx or Mailing cost = fixed cost + (cost per parcel × # or parcels)

A = fixed cost = $15,000 (from the picture – the Y intercept)

B = variable cost (slope) = ($75,000 − $15,000)/ ($20,000 − 0) = $3.00

The estimated cost for mailing 12,000 parcels is $15,000 + $3.00($12,000) = $51,000.

448. **Answer: D**

This is a detailed problem that requires working backwards through a contribution margin (CM) formatted income statement to determine total CM of $113,400. CM per unit ($5.25) is given by subtracting variable cost ($2.25) from price ($7.50). Year one units sold of 21,600 is calculated by dividing total CM ($113,400) by CM per unit ($5.25). Year two units sold (22,600 units) is equal to year one units plus 1,000 units.

449. **Answer: B**

This answer satisfies the basic breakeven quantity formula of fixed costs divided by contribution margin per unit (i.e., $360,000/$1,800).

450. **Answer: C**

This problem compares the increase in revenue due to the possible increased spending on advertising. The $15,000 for advertising is just another fixed cost. The contribution margin ratio is used to determine 40% of the new revenue of $780,000 = $312,000 resulting in only $12,000 more in contribution margin as compared to a new fixed advertising cost $15,000. The difference between the $15,000 and the $12,000 is a $3,000 decrease in income.

451. **Answer: B**

Absorption costing includes both variable and fixed manufacturing costs as product costs. Direct costing includes only variable manufacturing costs as product cost and expenses fixed manufacturing costs as a period expense.

In this case, absorption costing includes $20,000 of fixed manufacturing costs (1,000 × $20) in ending inventory while direct costing expenses the full amount of fixed manufacturing costs. Pretax income is consequently $20,000 higher for absorption costing.

452. Answer: B

Gross profit is the difference between sales and the cost of goods sold. The cost of goods sold includes fixed and variable manufacturing costs assigned to the units sold. Contribution margin equals sales less variable costs. Both the gross profit and the contribution margin are approximately as expected, which implies that sales, variable manufacturing costs, variable selling and administrative expenses, and fixed manufacturing costs are as expected. The only remaining component, fixed selling and administrative expenses, must be responsible for the variation in income.

453. Answer: D

Current ratio = current assets/current liabilities. Return on stockholders' equity = net income/average owners' equity. Absorption costing allocates both variable and fixed manufacturing costs to inventory. Variable costing assigns only variable manufacturing cost to inventory and expenses fixed manufacturing overhead as a period cost. Therefore, ending inventory, and thus, current assets, are higher under absorption costing by the amount of fixed overhead allocated to ending inventory. The current ratio under absorption costing is, therefore, higher than under variable costing. Income in the current period is the same under both absorption costing and variable costings because the fixed overhead allocation rate has not changed, and ending inventory quantities have not changed. Therefore, total expenses recognized for the life of the firm for absorption costing are less than for variable costing by the amount of fixed overhead remaining in those 5,000 units at the end of Year 2. Thus, retained earnings are higher for absorption costing, causing the denominator of return on stockholders' equity to be greater, and finally causing the ratio to be smaller for absorption costing.

454. Answer: C

Variable costs are presumed to be avoidable and fixed costs are presumed to be unavoidable to start with. Then $5,000 for rent was avoidable when they decided to buy. Thus, the cost to buy is $95,000 = $80,000 + $15,000 in fixed cost that are presumed unavoidable versus a cost to make of $90,000.

455. Answer: B

When the requirements of a specific job cause overtime to be incurred, the premium is incremental to that job and should be charged to it. A customer's immediate need for a product requiring personnel to stay overtime would be an example.

456. Answer: B

Ending balance in work in process:

$4,000 + $24,000 + $16,000 + $12,800 − $48,000 (all attributable to Job No. 5, the only remaining job) =	$8,800
Less direct labor charged to Job No. 5:	(2,000)
Less overhead charged to Job No. 5: .80($2,000)	(1,600)
Equals materials charged to Job No. 5:	$5,200

457. Answer: C

This answer is correct because (40,000 units * $5 materials cost * 100%) + (40,000 units * $7 conversion cost * 60%).

458. Answer: A

The FIFO method lets the costs and EUs associated with beginning WIP flow on to Finished Goods and bases the unit cost of production for the current period on the EUs started (and completed) during the period.

	Nominal Units	% Complete	Equivalent Units
Beginning WIP	10,000	30%	3,000
Units started and finished	130,000	100%	130,000
Ending WIP	20,000	25%	5,000
Units to account for or Equivalent units	160,000		138,000

459. Answer: A

Conversion costs include labor and overhead, and thus, are incurred continuously. The ending inventory would be 50% complete with respect to conversion costs. But material is added at the 60% point and the inventory is only 50% complete. Thus, no materials would be present in the ending inventory for this process.

These units would be the same as zero units with respect to material, for the purpose of costing ending inventory.

460. **Answer: B**

Acceptable joint cost allocation methods include sales value at split-off, physical measures, and constant gross margin. Flexible budget amounts are not used for joint cost allocation.

461. **Answer: D**

Using NRV, the final revenue for L is $8 (10,000 units produced) = $80,000; the final revenue for M is $20 (5,000 units produced) = $100,000; Sales less separable costs is $80,000 – $20,000 = $60,000 for L, while sales less separable costs for M is $100,000 – $40,000 = $60,000 for M also. Accordingly, both products have the same net realizable value, so the $36,000 in joint costs would be split 50/50 providing each with an allocation of $18,000.

462. **Answer: B**

The current method of accounting for May is to reduce the cost of goods sold of the major product by net sales of $3 per unit of May. The effect of this method of accounting is to increase gross margin by $3 per unit of May sold.

If the method of accounting were changed to joint product accounting, then sales would increase to $4 per unit of May sold, without any addition to variable cost. The $1 cost associated with each unit of May would be classified as a sales expense, which is subtracted below gross margin. The $1 expense would no longer affect gross margin. Therefore, by changing the method of accounting, the gross margin increases by $1, while expenses below gross margin in the income statement increase by $1. Gross margin would reflect the full $4 gross sales of May, rather than only the net reduction in the cost of goods sold of $3.

463. **Answer: B**

A direct efficiency variance is the difference between the actual quantity and the standard quantity allowed multiplied by the standard price. The variance is unfavorable because the actual quantity is greater than expected based on the standard.

464. **Answer: B**

To solve this we would use the formula (SP – AP) AQ. We are given SP and AP, but not AQ. We can find the AQ by dividing the actual total cost of $111,625 by the AP of $23.50 to get 4,750 hours. Now we multiply AQ of 4,750 by the $0.50 difference between the SP of $24 and the AP of $23.50 to get the price variance of $2,375. Since the actual price of $23.50 is less than the expected standard cost of $24, the variance is favorable.

465. **Answer: B**

The usage or quantity variance is calculated by using SP (SQA – AQ). Standard price (SP) is $5; actual quantity (AQ) is 25,000; and 20,000 is standard quantity allowed (SQA). This provides a 25,000-pound unfavorable usage variance of $25,000.

466. **Answer: C**

The spending variance is unaffected by the volume used for allocating the fixed overhead. The spending variance for the variable overhead is the difference between the actual overhead and the budgeted overhead based on actual direct labor hours. The spending variance for the fixed overhead is the difference between the actual overhead and the master budget for the fixed overhead. Neither variance is affected by the denominator used for allocating the fixed overhead.

However, the volume variance (computed for fixed overhead only) is the difference between the master budgeted fixed overhead and the allocated fixed overhead. The allocated fixed overhead is the product of the predetermined overhead rate per direct labor hour, and standard direct labor hours. An increase in the denominator of the predetermined fixed overhead rate from 80% to 100% of capacity would cause the predetermined overhead rate to decline, along with the allocated fixed overhead. This would increase the volume variance because the master budgeted fixed overhead would remain unchanged.

467. **Answer: B**

The variable overhead efficiency variance is computed only for variable overhead and equals:

(actual DL hours – standard DL hours)(standard variable overhead per DL hour) = [10,500 – 5,000(2)]($3) = $1,500.

In manufacturing 5,000 units, 10,000 direct labor hours should have been used at standard (5,000 units × 2 hours per unit). The actual number of hours used in the period was 500 more than this standard amount. At $3 standard variable overhead cost per direct labor, that means that $1,500 of variable overhead was incurred, because more direct labor hours were used than the standard.

468. **Answer: A**

The overhead volume variance equals the difference between the master budget for fixed overhead and applied fixed overhead. The variance has one cause only: producing a number of units different from that specified in the master budget. The variance can be broken down into the following:

(Master budget production volume – Actual production volume)(PF)(SQ)

where PF is the predetermined overhead rate for fixed overhead based on direct labor hours, and SQ is the standard quantity of direct labor hours per unit.

The production supervisor has less control over the actual production volume than the factors underlying the other variances listed, because actual production is strongly influenced by sales demand, a factor not under the control of the production supervisor. The supervisor has some responsibility for the volume level, however, when the volume falls below required levels due to maintenance and other internal problems. But typically, the volume variance is not one of the variances that is considered controllable by the production supervisor.

469. **Answer: C**

Sunk costs are resource costs that have already been incurred. These costs will not be changed as a result of current or future decision-making and, therefore, are not relevant when making financial (or other) decisions.

Opportunity costs are the benefits (e.g., revenues) given up when a selection of one course of action precludes another course of action (and the benefit it would have provided). As the name implies, these are the costs of forgoing one opportunity by choosing another opportunity.

470. **Answer: C**

Joint costs are sunk costs that are unavoidable, regardless of whether the item is sold at split-off or processed further.

471. **Answer: C**

This price covers the total variable cost of $9 and provides a contribution margin equal to that of the alternative use ($14 − $9 = $5 CM per unit; $5,000/1,000 units = $5 CM per unit).

472. **Answer: A**

With idle capacity, only the avoidable costs need to be covered. These include direct materials, direct labor, and avoidable fixed costs. These total $5.

473. **Answer: A**

Relevant costs to make and buy are correct, but without considering any additional information, since the cost to make is cheaper than the cost to buy, the prudent decision would be to make the rackets.

474. **Answer: B**

None of the applied fixed manufacturing costs should be considered, because the company has excess capacity, implying that the special job will not cause any additional fixed capacity costs to be incurred. Only the external design costs and variable costs are included, as only those costs are truly incremental and caused by the special job.

475. **Answer: C**

With the sale of tables, operating income will be reduced by the loss of the tables' contribution margin of $18,000. Also, $12,000 of avoidable fixed cost provided a relevant total decrease of $6,000 = ($18,000 − $12,000).

476. **Answer: D**

Following the general rule, the minimum transfer price (floor) is equal to the avoidable outlay costs, while the maximum transfer price (ceiling) is equal to the market price. However, this is only true where idle capacity exists to make the transfer. There is no idle capacity in case 2. Thus, the market value serves as both the ceiling and the floor for price. This value is $1.50.

477. **Answer: B**

Following the general rule, the minimum transfer price (floor) is equal to the avoidable outlay costs, while the maximum transfer price (ceiling) is equal to the market price. These values are $1.50 and $2.00, respectively.

478. Answer: B

In case 1, the floor of $1.50 and ceiling of $2.00 provide a viable range for the transfer to take place. Moreover, excess capacity allows for no service disruption to regular customers. In case 2, for the transfer to take place, the units necessary would need to be denied from regular customers, since no excess capacity exists; thus, the transfer will likely not take place.

479. Answer: B

Standard variable cost is preferable. The "variable" part of the cost description results in passing to the purchasing division only the incremental costs of the item. The purchasing division should not pay for the fixed costs of the selling division unless the order caused those fixed costs to increase (which is not implied by the question's data). The "standard" part of the cost description makes sure that the purchasing division is not charged for inefficiencies in the selling division.

The question does not contain sufficient information to deviate from a commonly used rule for setting transfer prices: standard variable cost + lost contribution margin to seller.

480. Answer: C

Employee benefits expense provides no clear relationship to the manufacturing operations portion of the company. At least the other allocation bases have some relationship to the manufacturing process.

481. Answer: C

Both I. and III. are common characteristics of the ABC approach.

For the purpose of cost estimation and allocation. Single variables such as direct labor hours or machine hours are not used, but rather, multiple variables are identified (which could include the latter two), in an effort to identify the underlying relationship between cost and its causes. Also, nonvalue-added activities are identified and eliminated or reduced. Inventories are typically reduced along with the related storage and security activities, and paperwork and other activities that do not add value to the product are minimized. However, II. is not a characteristic of ABC systems. II. is a statement of the way overhead costs are allocated in traditional costing systems. ABC

disaggregates overhead costs into specific activities or drivers, computes overhead rates for each driver, and then allocates overhead to products based on their consumption or the use of the driver. Thus, ABC first allocates overhead to activities and then to products, rather than to departments and then to products, as is the case with traditional systems.

482. Answer: D

A value-added activity is one that makes the product or service more valuable to the customer.

The only activity listed in the answer Alternatives that adds no value to the product or service as perceived by the customer is raw materials storage.

ABC systems and JIT purchasing systems are frequently used together. One objective is to minimize inventory holdings. The level of inventory held has no bearing on product quality or the satisfaction of the customer. By reducing inventories, less material must be stored, reducing all the attendant activities and costs related to material storage. Thus, the total cost is reduced without affecting the customer and sales.

483. Answer: C

ABC systems increase (rather than eliminate) the number of cost drivers, to enable better modeling of cost along cause-effect lines. Cost drivers are explanatory variables that help to explain the behavior of cost. One or two independent variables typically are insufficient to explain the behavior of many indirect manufacturing costs.

ABC systems also seek to eliminate nonvalue-added activities, which are activities that do not add to the value of the product as perceived by the customer. In so doing, the total cost of producing the product is reduced without any effect on the value of the product.

484. Answer: D

ABC systems identify more cost drivers (allocation bases) than traditional costing systems do. Cost drivers are independent variables that help to explain the behavior of cost and are, therefore, useful in providing cost allocations that more closely reflect the causal factors affecting cost behavior. Costs are divided into a greater number of cost pools for this purpose, to group together those costs that behave similarly and that may be related to smaller production cells. The number of different costs in each pool is smaller than is the case for traditional systems, which may aggregate costs by department or product line.

485. **Answer: A**

Volume-based production is somewhat of an opposite to activity-based costing in the sense that the volume-based approach, while simple, does not accurately reflect the relationship between the products produced and the costs incurred, as it systematically overassigns costs to some products and underassigns costs to others.

486. **Answer: A**

A company would most benefit from using ABC when indirect costs are a high percentage of total costs. This is due to the fact indirect costs must be allocated while direct cost assignments are traceable.

487. **Answer: B**

Since the desired ending inventory is 15 units more than the beginning inventory, production must be 15 units greater than the projected sales level of 1,000 units.

488. **Answer: B**

Gross Profit ($70,000) is determined by subtracting Cost of Goods Sold ($350,000) from Sales ($420,000). Sales is calculated by multiplying a markup of 20% based on cost of goods sold (i.e., $420,000 = 1.2($350,000). Cost of Goods Sold is easily determined by using an accounts payable T-account to calculate purchases of $350,000 by using the cash paid of $300,000 and the beginning and ending balances of accounts payable ($100,000 and $150,000, respectively).

489. **Answer: B**

Variable cost per office	= ($500,000 − $70,000)/5
	= $86,000
Total estimated cost of seven offices	= $86,000(7) + $70,000 (fixed cost)
	= $672,000

490. **Answer: D**

First, purchases must be computed, and then the estimated payments to be made on accounts payable. With inventory declining, purchases must equal cost of sales less the decline in inventory. In other words, purchases are less than cost of sales if inventory declines. If the gross margin is 40% of sales, then cost of sales is 60% of sales.

Purchases	= Cost of sales − Inventory decline
	= (.60)($2,800,000) − $70,000
	= $1,610,000

If accounts payable (AP) is to decrease, payments on AP must exceed purchases. Estimated payments on AP = $1,610,000 + $150,000 decrease in AP = $1,760,000.

491. **Answer: C**

Flexible budgets are budgets produced at different activity levels. Direct material usage budgets are commonly prepared for different activity levels to indicate the level of cost that should be incurred at those levels. The actual cost is then compared with the budget for the level of activity actually attained. The comparison is much more relevant for evaluation purposes than would be the comparison between the actual and the master or static budgets if the level of activity in the master and static budgets were not the same.

The same idea applies for marketing cost, although there typically is less "flex" in this type of budgeted cost. A good proportion of the marketing cost is fixed. Other portions are variable (e.g., commissions). Both costs, however, can be expressed as part of a flexible budget. Many flexible budgets include fixed components. The term "flexible" budget does not imply the exclusion of fixed costs.

492. **Answer: D**

The constant, a, in a regression equation to calculate cost depicts the total fixed cost.

493. **Answer: D**

Total cost (y) is expressed as $90 of variable cost per unit + $45 of fixed cost. Given that x represents units, we solve for $y = \$90(100) + \$45 = \$9,045$.

494. **Answer: B**

The coefficient of determination, identified as R^2 (R-squared), indicates the degree to which the behavior of the independent variable(s) predicts or explains the dependent variable.

495. **Answer: B**

The independent variable (x) is the one that is believed to have a causal effect on cost, the dependent variable (y). The variable is called "independent" because its level is first set in order to determine the effect on cost. For example, x might be output level. The firm is interested in determining the effect of different outputs (set first) on cost (determined second). Cost is "dependent" on the independent variable output.

496. **Answer: B**

There are two states of nature that can affect the firm's earnings: frost and no frost. There are also two actions under consideration: provide frost protection for $10,000, or do not. The expected income under each action will depend on the probability of frost. Let p = the probability of frost. Expected net income if frost protection is provided = $90,000(p) + $60,000(1 − p) − $10,000. Expected net income if frost protection is not provided = $40,000(p) + $60,000(1 − p). The firm is indifferent between the two actions when the expected net income is the same for both. Setting the two expressions equal to each other and solving for p determines at what probability of frost the two actions provide the same income.

$$\$90,000(p) + \$60,000(1 - p) - \$10,000 = \$40,000(p) + \$60,000(1 - p)$$
$$\$50,000(p) = \$10,000$$
$$p = .20$$

When the probability of frost exceeds .20, the expected income from providing frost protection exceeds that of not providing frost protection. This can be verified by entering a probability higher than .20 into both income expressions and determining the income. This is the expected result. As the probability of frost increases, the expected benefits of providing frost protection also increase.

The opposite is true for probabilities lower than .20.

497. **Answer: B**

Coefficient of determination measures goodness of fit.

498. **Answer: C**

Neither trade accounts payable nor inventories are considered long-term issues; capital budgeting is considered a long-term issue.

499. **Answer: A**

Financial management is concerned with decisions and activities that deal with both short-term and long-term matters.

500. **Answer: B**

Dividend policy is a long-term financial management activity or concern.

Written Communications and Task-Based Simulations

Economic Concepts and Analysis

International Economics

Business Strategy and Market Analysis: Generic Strategies

1. Written Communication

TBSBWB0141

Written communication	
	Help

The chief executive officer of Urton Corp., Geroge Jones, is preparing for a strategic planning session with the corporation's board of directors. The company has pursued a product differentiation strategy in the past but is having difficulty maintaining margins due to significant competition from domestic and foreign competitors. Write a memorandum describing the product differentiation strategy and another strategy that might be pursued if product differentiation is not working.

REMINDER:

Your response will be graded for both technical content and writing skills. Technical content will be evaluated for information that is helpful to the intended reader and clearly relevant to the issue. Writing skills will be evaluated for development, organization, and the appropriate expression of ideas in professional correspondence. Use a standard business memo or letter format with a clear beginning, middle, and end. Do not convey information in the form of a table, bullet point list, or other abbreviated presentation.

Upon completion of your memo, click SAVE and evaluate your response against the suggested response.

Scoring Reference: In the Wiley CPAexcel grading software for written communication tasks, of the 100 possible points, how would you score your response? Consider the following:

- Technical content: Is your content relevant, on-topic, and helpful to the intended user? (suggest 0–50 points)

- Writing skills: Is your content organized, developed, and are your ideas expressed appropriately (e.g., grammar, punctuation, and spelling)? (suggest 0–50 points)

---

1. Written Communication Solution

Written communication	
	Help

TO: Mr. George Jones, CEO Urton Corp.

From: CPA Candidate

As you requested, this memorandum is designed to discuss some alternative strategies that may be implemented by Urton Corp. Historically, Urton has implemented a product differentiation strategy. This strategy involves providing products that have superior physical characteristics, perceived differences, or support service differences, which allows the products to command higher prices in the market. When effective, this strategy allows the company to effectively compete with companies that sell lower priced products.

For a product differentiation strategy to be successful, the company must continue to invest in the differentiating factor. Since Urton is no longer effectively competing using a product differentiating strategy, the management should consider whether additional investment in product innovation, support services, or brand identity might allow the company to revive the strategy.

On the other hand, if management believes that pursuing a differentiation strategy is no longer feasible, consideration should be given to a cost leadership strategy. Pursuing a cost leadership strategy would involve cutting costs and improving efficiency to allow the company to offer products at lower prices.

To be competitive, it is essential that the company select a strategy and begin to align management's decisions with that strategy. If you need any additional information, please contact me.

Microeconomics

Market Structure and Firm Strategy: Summary of Market Structure

2. Task-Based Simulation

tbs.aq.mkstrct.smmry_001.2017

Work Tab	
	Help

Rod Harvey, a successful local businessman and major client of your firm, has discussed with Joe Counts, the partner in charge of Mr. Harvey's accounts with the firm, his desire to open a restaurant in the local community. In his discussions with Mr. Counts, Mr. Harvey said he is considering two different styles of restaurants and that he would like an analysis of each of those alternatives.

The first possibility he is considering is a high-end steakhouse that would cater to individuals and groups seeking a fine-dining experience. The restaurant would serve the highest-quality meats available exclusively from an international supplier as well as premium wines and distilled products. Mr. Harvey believes that such a restaurant would be successful because there are only two other first-class steakhouses in the area and because he would have an exclusive area-wide right to acquire goods from the acclaimed international supplier.

The other possibility Mr. Harvey is considering is a family-oriented casual dining restaurant. Such a restaurant would compete with a number of existing restaurants, both locally owned and franchised. Mr. Harvey believes such a restaurant would be successful because of the high demand for reasonably priced, casual dining in the area and because his business experience would permit him to manage operations better than his competition.

Based on the information provided by Mr. Harvey and his own understanding of economics, Mr. Counts concluded that the two types of restaurants being considered would operate in different market structures. The steakhouse proposal would operate in an oligopolistic market and the family-oriented restaurant in a monopolistic competitive market. Further, he believes that the requested analysis should include consideration of the different markets.

Mr. Counts assigns responsibility for drafting the economic markets section of the report to a summer intern, May Askew, and directs you to review and revise her draft before submitting it for inclusion in the final report. Specifically, he wants that section of the report to identify the characteristics of the two market structures, oligopoly and monopolistic competition, and briefly describe the strategy considerations for each type of market.

May Askew's draft report is presented below. You are to review and, if needed, correct Ms. Askew's draft report.

TO: Mr. Joe Counts, Partner

FROM: May Askew, Summer Intern

SUBJECT: Market Structures Section of Harvey Restaurant Analysis

The following provides the material for the market structures section of the restaurant analysis being prepared for Mr. Harvey. Specifically, it defines the characteristics of the two market structures in which the proposed restaurant types would operate and briefly describes the business strategy considerations for each of those markets.

Introduction

From the perspective of the providers of a good or service, a market consists of those firm that compete with each other for customers of the good or service. The structure of a market is determined primarily by the number of firms in a market, the extent to which their product or service differs from those offered by others in the market, and the ease with which firms can enter and leave the market. Based on the information you provided and our own analysis, we have concluded that each of the restaurant types you are considering would operate in separate economic market structures. Specifically, we conclude that a steakhouse restaurant would operate in an oligopoly market and a family-oriented, casual dining restaurant would operate in a monopolistic competitive market. Each of these markets and related strategy considerations are described in the following subsection.

	(A)	(B)	(C)	(D)	(E)	(F)
1. Steakhouse Restaurant We conclude that a steakhouse restaurant in our community would operate in an oligopolistic market. A. An oligopolistic market is one that is characterized by having only a few sellers that sell either the same good or service or a somewhat different good or service and where it is easy to enter the market. B. An oligopolistic market is one that is characterized by having many sellers that sell the same good or service and where it is easy to enter the market. C. An oligopolistic market is one that is characterized by having many sellers that sell only the same good or service and where it is difficult to enter the market. D. An oligopolistic market is one that is characterized by having only a few sellers that sell only different goods or services and where it is easy to enter the market. E. An oligopolistic market is one that is characterized by having only a few sellers that sell either the same good or service or a somewhat different good or service and where it is difficult to enter the market. F. An oligopolistic market is one that is characterized by having only a few sellers that sell only different goods or services and where it is difficult to enter the market.	○	○	○	○	○	○
2. The characteristics of an oligopoly market have direct implications for a firm that operates in such a market. Specifically, firms in an oligopoly market must focus considerable strategic attention on the actions and anticipated actions of other firms in the market in order to stay competitive. A. The firms tend to engage in price competition and use nonprice competition, including focusing on the quality of their good/service, customer relations, loyalty programs, and the like. B. The firms tend to engage primarily in price competition in order to increase market share. C. The firms tend to engage in price competition but normally avoid nonprice competition. D. The firms tend to avoid price competition and rather compete on factors other than price, including the quality of their good/service, customer relations, loyalty programs, and the like. E. The firms tend to avoid any form of competition.	○	○	○	○	○	○

	(A)	(B)	(C)	(D)	(E)	(F)
3. Family-Oriented, Casual Dining Restaurant	○	○	○	○	○	○

3. **Family-Oriented, Casual Dining Restaurant**
We conclude that a family-oriented, casual dining restaurant in our community would operate in a monopolistic competitive market.
   A. A monopolistic competitive market is characterized by having many sellers that sell a distinctive product for which there are no close substitutes and where it is easy to enter the market.
   B. A monopolistic competitive market is characterized by having few sellers that sell a distinctive product for which there are no close substitutes and where it is easy to enter the market.
   C. A monopolistic competitive market is characterized by having many sellers that sell a homogenous product and where it is easy to enter the market.
   D. A monopolistic competitive market is characterized by having many sellers that sell a distinctive product for which there are close substitutes and where it is easy to enter the market.
   E. A monopolistic competitive market is characterized by having a few sellers that sell a homogenous product and where it is easy to enter the market.
   F. A monopolistic competitive market is characterized by having many sellers that sell a distinctive product and where it is difficult to enter the market.

| 4. As is true of other market structures, the characteristics of monopolistic | ○ | ○ | ○ | ○ | ○ | ○ |

4. As is true of other market structures, the characteristics of monopolistic completion have direct implications for the formulation of business strategy.
   A. Firms in a monopolistic competitive market tend to avoid price competition and commonly attempt to differentiate their product or service by using nonprice forms of competition.
   B. Firms in a monopolistic competitive market tend to avoid any form of competition.
   C. Firms in a monopolistic competitive market tend to engage in price competition but tend to avoid other forms of competition.
   D. Firms in a monopolistic competitive market tend to engage in both price competition and nonprice forms of competition.

Summary and Conclusion

The two restaurant types being considered would operate in different market structures. An understanding of these market structures provides insight not only into the difference in the markets but also into certain business strategies appropriate for each market.

2. Task-Based Simulation Solution

Work Tab	
	Help

		(A)	(B)	(C)	(D)	(E)	(F)
1.	**Steakhouse Restaurant**	○	○	○	○	●	○

We conclude that a steakhouse restaurant in our community would operate in an oligopolistic market.

A. An oligopolistic market is one that is characterized by having only a few sellers that sell either the same good or service or a somewhat different good or service and where it is easy to enter the market.

B. An oligopolistic market is one that is characterized by having many sellers that sell the same good or service and where it is easy to enter the market.

C. An oligopolistic market is one that is characterized by having many sellers that sell only the same good or service and where it is difficult to enter the market.

D. An oligopolistic market is one that is characterized by having only a few sellers that sell only different goods or services and where it is easy to enter the market.

E. An oligopolistic market is one that is characterized by having only a few sellers that sell either the same good or service or a somewhat different good or service and where it is difficult to enter the market.

F. An oligopolistic market is one that is characterized by having only a few sellers that sell only different goods or services and where it is difficult to enter the market.

		(A)	(B)	(C)	(D)	(E)	(F)
2.		○	○	○	●	○	○

2. The characteristics of an oligopoly market have direct implications for a firm that operates in such a market. Specifically, firms in an oligopoly market must focus considerable strategic attention on the actions and anticipated actions of other firms in the market in order to stay competitive.

A. The firms tend to engage in price competition and use nonprice competition, including focusing on the quality of their good/service, customer relations, loyalty programs, and the like.

B. The firms tend to engage primarily in price competition in order to increase market share.

C. The firms tend to engage in price competition but normally avoid nonprice competition.

D. The firms tend to avoid price competition and rather compete on factors other than price, including the quality of their good/service, customer relations, loyalty programs, and the like.

E. The firms tend to avoid any form of competition.

	(A)	(B)	(C)	(D)	(E)	(F)

3. Family-Oriented, Casual Dining Restaurant   ○ ○ ○ ● ○ ○
We conclude that a family-oriented, casual dining restaurant in our
community would operate in a monopolistic competitive market.
   A. A monopolistic competitive market is characterized by having many
       sellers that sell a distinctive product for which there are no close
       substitutes and where it is easy to enter the market.
   B. A monopolistic competitive market is characterized by having few
       sellers that sell a distinctive product for which there are no close
       substitutes and where it is easy to enter the market.
   C. A monopolistic competitive market is characterized by having many
       sellers that sell a homogenous product and where it is easy to enter
       the market.
   D. A monopolistic competitive market is characterized by having
       many sellers that sell a distinctive product for which there are close
       substitutes and where it is easy to enter the market.
   E. A monopolistic competitive market is characterized by having a few
       sellers that sell a homogenous product and where it is easy to enter
       the market.
   F. A monopolistic competitive market is characterized by having many
       sellers that sell a distinctive product and where it is difficult to enter
       the market.

4. As is true of other market structures, the characteristics of monopolistic   ○ ○ ○ ● ○ ○
   completion have direct implications for the formulation of business
   strategy.
   A. Firms in a monopolistic competitive market tend to avoid price
       competition and commonly attempt to differentiate their product or
       service by using nonprice forms of competition.
   B. Firms in a monopolistic competitive market tend to avoid any form of
       competition.
   C. Firms in a monopolistic competitive market tend to engage in price
       competition but tend to avoid other forms of competition.
   D. Firms in a monopolistic competitive market tend to engage in both
       price competition and nonprice forms of competition.

Answers and Explanations

1. **(E)** This answer is correct. An oligopolistic market is one that is characterized by having only a few
    sellers that sell either the same good or service or a somewhat different good or service and where it is
    difficult to enter the market.
2. **(D)** This answer is correct. Because there are few firms in the market, each firm is aware of the actions
    taken by other firms. Therefore, if one firm lowers its price in an effort to increase market share, other
    firms will respond by lowering their prices, which could result in a price war. As a consequence, firms
    in an oligopolistic market tend to avoid price competition and instead focus on nonprice forms of
    competition, including the quality of their good/service, customer relations, loyalty programs, and the
    like.
3. **(D)** This answer is correct. A monopolistic competitive market is characterized by having many sellers
    that sell a distinctive product for which there are close substitutes and where it is easy to enter the
    market.
4. **(D)** This answer is correct. Firms in a monopolistic competitive market tend to engage in both price
    competition and nonprice forms of competition, including the extensive use of advertising and
    customer relations programs.

Capital Budgeting

Evaluation Techniques: Net Present Value Approach

3. Task-Based Simulation

tbs.aq.ss.netprs.valappr.04_17

Work Tab	
	Help

Bizco, Inc. is currently considering implementing two capital projects: (1) an upgrade to one of its production lines and (2) establishing its own waste disposal site. The specifications for both possible projects have been prepared and the expected costs and benefits of each project have been determined. A Project Estimation Summary for each of the projects is provided in the Exhibits above (Project 17-06 Summary and Project 17-07 Summary).

Project 17-06 Summary

Bizco, Inc.   Project Estimation Summary   Project #: 17-06_

Estimator: W.R. Jordan   Estimation Date: 10/23/2017   Start Date: 1/2/2018

Project Short Title: Production Line #3 upgrade

Project Brief Description: Automation upgrade to production line #3 is intended to increase___ annual output and reduce production costs.

Expected Project Life: 5 Years   Current Weighted Average Cost of Capital: 10%

ESTIMATED CASH COSTS:	ESTIMATED CASH BENEFITS:
Initial Fixed Asset (F/A) Investment $120,000	Annual Cash Inflows:[1]
	Year(s) ___1 - 5___ Amount $ 20,000
Initial Working Capital	Year(s) _____ Amount $_____
(W/C) Investment .... $ 20,000	Year(s) _____ Amount $_____
Subsequent Investment(s)	
Year(s) ___-___ Amount $__-__	Annual Cash Savings:[2]
Year(s) ___-___ Amount $__-__	Year(s) ___1 - 3___ Amount $ 20,000
	Year(s) __4 & 5__ Amount $ 15,000
	Year(s) _____ Amount $_____
End of Project Remediation Cost	F/A Residual/Salvage Value
Year(s) ___-___ Amount $__-__	Year(s) ___5___ Amount $ 5,000
	W/C Residual Value
	Year(s) ___5___ Amount $ 20,000

Project 17-07 Summary

Bizco, Inc.   Project Estimation Summary   Project #: 17-07

Estimator: W.R. Jordan Estimation Date: 11/06/2017 Start Date: 1/2/2018

Project Short Title: Development of company waste disposal site

Project Brief Description: Acquistion and development of a company-owned waste disposal site to replace current contracted waste disposal.

Expected Project Life: 10 Years   Current Weighted Average Cost of Capital: 10%

ESTIMATED CASH COSTS:	ESTIMATED CASH BENEFITS:
Initial Fixed Asset (F/A) Investment[1] $300,000	Annual Cash Inflows: Year(s) _____ Amount $_____ Year(s) _____ Amount $_____ Year(s) _____ Amount $_____
Initial Working Capital Investment $ -	
Subsequent Investment(s)[2] Year(s) 1 - 9 Amount $ 5,000 Year(s) - Amount $ -	Annual Cash Savings: Year(s) 1 - 10 Amount $ 60,000 Year(s) _____ Amount $_____ Year(s) _____ Amount $_____
End of Project Remediation Cost[3] Year(s) 10 Amount $ 40,000	F/A Residual/Salvage Value[4] Year(s) 10 Amount $ 25,000
	W/C Residual Value Year(s) _____ Amount $_____

FOOTNOTES/COMMENTS: [1]Initial F/A investment includes the acquisition of land and its development as a disposal site.

You have been assigned the responsibility of analyzing each project to determine whether or not it is economically feasible and, using assumed net present values, to determine which project will provide the better return for the amount invested.

In addition to the project estimation summaries, you are provided present value and future value tables in the following exhibits.

P/V of Single Amount

Present Value of a Single Sum ($1)

n	2%	4%	6%	8%	10%
1	0.980	0.962	0.843	0.926	0.909
2	0.961	0.925	0.890	0.857	0.826
3	0.942	0.889	0.840	0.794	0.751
4	0.924	0.855	0.792	0.735	0.683
5	0.906	0.822	0.747	0.681	0.621
6	0.888	0.790	0.705	0.630	0.564
7	0.871	0.760	0.665	0.583	0.513
8	0.853	0.731	0.627	0.540	0.467
9	0.837	0.703	0.592	0.500	0.424
10	0.820	0.676	0.558	0.463	0.386

F/V of Single Amount

Future Value of a Single Sum ($1)

n	2%	4%	6%	8%	10%
1	1.020	1.040	1.060	1.080	1.100
2	1.040	1.082	1.124	1.166	1.210
3	1.061	1.125	1.191	1.260	1.331
4	1.082	1.170	1.262	1.360	1.464
5	1.104	1.217	1.338	1.469	1.611
6	1.126	1.265	1.419	1.587	1.772
7	1.149	1.316	1.504	1.714	1.949
8	1.172	1.369	1.594	1.851	2.144
9	1.195	1.423	1.689	1.999	2.358
10	1.218	1.480	1.791	2.159	2.594

P/V of Ordinary Annuity

Present Value of Ordinary Annuity

n	2%	4%	6%	8%	10%
1	0.980	0.962	0.943	0.926	0.909
2	1.942	1.885	1.833	1.783	1.736
3	2.884	2.775	2.673	2.577	2.487
4	3.808	3.630	3.465	3.312	3.170
5	4.713	4.452	4.212	3.993	3.791
6	5.601	5.242	4.917	4.623	4.355
7	6.472	6.002	5.582	5.206	4.968
8	7.325	6.733	6.210	5.747	5.335
9	8.162	7.435	6.802	6.247	5.759
10	8.963	8.111	7,360	6.710	6.145

F/V of Ordinary Annuity

Future Value of Ordinary Annuity

n	2%	4%	6%	8%	10%
1	1.000	1.000	1.000	1.000	1.000
2	2.020	2.040	2.060	2.080	2.100
3	3.060	3.122	3.184	3.246	3.310
4	4.122	4.246	4.375	4.506	4.641
5	5.204	5.416	5.637	5.867	6.105
6	6.308	6.633	6.975	7.336	7.716
7	7.434	7.898	8.394	8.923	9.487
8	8.583	9.241	9.897	10.637	11.436
9	9.755	10.583	11.491	12.488	13.579
10	10.950	12.006	13.181	14.487	15.937

The results of your analysis are to be provided by responding to each of the following questions:

A. For Project 17-06

Enter the appropriate amount in column B. Round to the nearest dollar.

What is the present value of estimated total cash outflows?	
What is the present value of estimated cash flow benefit from additional product sales?	
What is the total present value of estimated cash flow benefit from reduced production costs?	
What is the total present value of estimated cash flow benefit from residual values?	
What is the NET present value (NPV) of estimated cash flows for the project?	

Click the cell in column B and select from the list.

	(A)	(B)
Based on your analysis, is this project (17-06) economically feasible?	○	○

A. Yes
B. No

B. For Project 17-07

Enter the appropriate amount in the column B. Round to the nearest dollar.

What is the total present value of estimated total cash outflows?	
What is the total present value of estimated annual cash benefits from all project sources?	
What is the NET present value (NPV) of estimated cash flows for the project?	

Click the cell in column B and select from the list.

	(A)	(B)
Based on your analysis, is this project (17-07) economically feasible?	○	○

A. Yes
B. No

C. Assume the following are the net present values for each of the projects:

Project 17-06 NPV = $20,000

Project 17-07 NPV = $30,000

If the net present value and only the initial investment(s) of each project are considered in the analysis, using the profitability index, which one of the projects should be selected as providing the best benefit to cost?

Click the associated cell in column B and select from the list.

	(A)	(B)
Project Selected	○	○

A. Project 17-06
B. Project 17-07

3. Task-Based Simulation Solution

Work Tab	
	Help

What is the present value of estimated total cash outflows?	$140,000
What is the present value of estimated cash flow benefit from additional product sales?	$75,820
What is the total present value of estimated cash flow benefit from reduced production costs?	$69,300
What is the total present value of estimated cash flow benefit from residual values?	$15,525
What is the NET present value (NPV) of estimated cash flows for the project?	$20,645

	(A)	(B)
Based on your analysis, is this project (17-06) economically feasible?	●	○

A. Yes
B. No

What is the total present value of estimated total cash outflows?	$344,235
What is the total present value of estimated annual cash benefits from all project sources?	$378,350
What is the NET present value (NPV) of estimated cash flows for the project?	$34,115

	(A)	(B)
Based on your analysis, is this project (17-07) economically feasible?	●	○

A. Yes
B. No

	(A)	(B)
Project Selected	●	○

A. Project 17-06
B. Project 17-07

Present Value from Estimated Total Cash Outflows

The present value of estimated total cash outflow is $140,000. All cash outflows occur at the initiation of the project and are at present value. Therefore, the sum of the initial F/A investment and the initial W/C investment constitute the total cash outflow. Those amounts are (F/A) $120,000 + (W/C) $20,000 = $140,000.

Present Value from Additional Product Sales

The present value of estimated cash flow benefit from additional product sales is $75,820. The cash flow benefit from additional product sales is the annual cash inflow of $20,000 for the 5 years of the project. Since the cash inflow is uniform over the 5-year period ($20,000 each year), the cash flow is an annuity. The PV factor for an annuity for 5 years at 10% is 3.791. Therefore, the PV of the $20,000 annual additional sales is $20,000 × 3.791 = $75,820.

Total Present Value from Reduced Production Costs

The total present value of estimated cash flow benefit from reduced production costs is $69,300. The cash flow benefit from reduced production cost is $20,000 per year for years 1–3 and $15,000 per year for years

4 and 5. Since the cash flows for years 1–3 are uniform over that period ($20,000), it is an annuity for 3 years. Thus, the PV for an annuity factor can be used. Since the cash flow for years 4 and 5 are not the same amount ($15,000) as for years 1–3, those two years are not part of the annuity. Their present values can be determined by getting the PV of a single amount for 4 years and, separately, for 5 years. The relevant PV factors and calculated PVs are:

Years 1–3	$20,000 × (PV of annuity for 3 years @ 10%) 2.487 = $ 49,740
Year 4	$15,000 × (PV of single amount for 4 years @ 10%) 0.683 = 10,245
Year 5	$15,000 × (PV of single amount for 5 years @ 10%) 0.621 = 9,315
TOTAL PV OF REDUCED PRODUCTION COSTS	$69,300

Total Present Value from Residual Values

The total present value of estimated cash flow benefit from residual values is $15,525. The cash flow from residual values includes the residual values from disposal of the fixed asset investment and from the recovery of the working capital investment. Both residual values are single amounts; therefore, the PV of both will be determined using PV of a single amount. The relevant PV factors and calculated PVs are:

Fixed asset	Year 5	$5,000 × (PV of $1) 0.621	=	$3,105
Working capital	Year 5	$20,000 × (PV of $1) 0.621	=	12,420
TOTAL PV OF RESIDUAL VALUES				$15,525

Net Present Value

The NET present value (NPV) of estimated cash flows for the project is $20,645. Net present value (NPV) of a project is determined as the PV of cash inflows (benefits) less the PV of cash outflows (investments/costs). If the net is zero or positive (PV of cash inflows ≥ PV of cash outflows), the project is economically feasible. For project 17-06 the PV of cash inflows and cash outflows are:

Inflows (computed above):	
PV of additional sales	$75,820
PV of annual savings	69,300
PV of residual values	15,525
Total PV of Inflows	$160,645
Less: Cash Outflows	
(computed above)	
PV of initial investments	140,000
NET PRESENT VALUE	$20,645

Yes, the project 17-06 is economically feasible. The present value of the expected cash inflows exceeds the present value of expected cash outflows by $20,645; the project has a positive net present value.

Total Present Value of Estimated Total Cash Flows

The total present value of estimated total cash outflows is $344,235.

Project cash outflows come from three uses: (1) the initial investment, which is for land and its development; (2) subsequent annual investments for 9 years for the installation of monitoring equipment for the disposal site; and (3) remediation costs required at the end of the project life to reinstate the land to an acceptable condition. The initial investment is at present value, but the subsequent investments and remediation cost have to be discounted to present value. The subsequent investments are of equal amounts for 9 years; therefore, they constitute an annuity, which would be discounted using the PV of an annuity factor. The remediation cost is at the end of the project life, so it is a one-time payment that would be discounted using the PV of a single amount factor. The relevant present value factors and resulting present value amounts are:

Initial investment in F/A (@PV)		$300,000
Subsequent investments	$5,000 × (annuity 9 years @10%) 5.759	28,795
Remediation costs	$40,000 × (PV $1 for 10 years @10%) 0.386	15,440
Total Present Value of Cash Outflows		$344,235

Total present value of estimated annual cash benefits from all project sources

What is the total present value of estimated annual cash benefits from all project sources? $378,350

The cash benefits of the project derive from cash savings and the residual value of the land at the end of the life of the project. The annual cash savings for the 10-year life of the project is $60,000. Since it is the same amount each year, it is an annuity, and its present value can be determined using the PV of an annuity factor. The residual value of the land will be received at the end of the 10-year life of the project; therefore, it is a single payment, and its present value can be determined using the PV of a single amount factor. The relevant table factors and present values are:

Cash savings	$60,000 × (annuity for 10 years @10%) 6.145	$368,700
Residual value of land	$25,000 × (PV of $1 for 10 years @ 10%) 0.386	9,650
Total present value of project benefits (flows)		$378,350

NET present value (NPV) of estimated cash flows for the project

The NET present value (NPV) of estimated cash flows for the project is $34,115.

The net present value of estimated cash flows/benefits is computed as the PV of cash inflows/benefits less the PV of cash outflows/costs. For this project, those values (computed above) are:

PV of cash inflows/benefits	$378,350
PV of cash outflows/costs	344,235
Net cash flow of project (positive)	$34,115

The project is economically feasible because the PV of net cash flow from the project is positive; the PV of cash inflows is greater than the PV of cash outflows by $34,115.

The profitability index (PI) ranks projects by determining the expected return on each dollar invested. It can be computed either as: (1) PV of Cash Inflows/Initial Investment, or (2) NPV/Initial Investment. The requirement is to use the NPV of each project as given in the facts and the initial investment(s) only. The respective calculations are:

(A) Project 17-06 PI = NPV > $20,000/Initial Investment > $140,000 = .1429

(A) Project 17-07 PI = NPV > $30,000/Initial Investment > $300,000 = .1000

When the NPV is used, the resulting PI would be ≥ 0, which means the project is providing value at least equal to the discount rate (e.g., WACC) used to get present values. The resulting percentage index (≥ 0) for each project can be used to rank projects; the higher the percentage, the higher the rank of the project. Therefore, Project 17-06 with an index of .1429, which is greater than the index for Project 17-07 (.1000), would provide a greater return per dollar invested.

Information Technology

Processing Integrity (Input/Processing/Output Controls)

Processing, File, and Output Controls

4. Task-Based Simulation

tbs.it.appctrl.proc.001_2017

Work Tab	
	Help

In preparation for their annual audit, ABC Company decided to look over their order-to-cash process. They identified some vulnerabilities, listed below. Match the vulnerability with the control that they should implement or tighten, and indicate if that control is an input and origination control or an output control.

For each scenario, click in the associated cells and select from the lists provided the correct answers. A selection may be used once, more than once, or not at all.

Scenario	Control				Input or Output	
	(A)	**(B)**	**(C)**	**(D)**	**(A)**	**(B)**
1. Susan and Sarah are the only sales reps at ABC company, but when they get behind, they ask Paul, the purchasing intern to help take customer calls and create sales orders. He's not on their team, but they figure that it's good experience for Paul, and they need the help, anyway. A. All reports and documentation that may contain sensitive data should be disposed of using secure disposal techniques. B. All items that are sold should have a bar code that can be scanned. C. All workstations should have authorization and identification controls, and employees should be trained to not share passwords. D. Sales transactions should be backed and logged immediately as transactions occur. A. Input and Origination Controls B. Output Controls	○	○	○	○	○	○

	Scenario	Control				Input or Output	
		(A)	(B)	(C)	(D)	(A)	(B)
2.	Susan has a tendency to forget the inventory ID for some of the items that they don't sell too frequently. She tries to look them up every time, but sometimes she gets in a hurry and makes a guess. This results in some sales orders having the wrong inventory ID for what was actually sold. A. All reports and documentation that may contain sensitive data should be disposed of using secure disposal techniques. B. All items that are sold should have a bar code that can be scanned. C. All workstations should have authorization and identification controls, and employees should be trained to not share passwords. D. Sales transactions should be backed and logged immediately as transactions occur. A. Input and Origination Controls B. Output Controls	○	○	○	○	○	○
3.	Greg, the database administrator, is supposed to be responsible for implementing a disaster recovery plan, but he's been extremely short-staffed lately. Even though the disaster recovery plan is documented and the sales system should be backed up weekly, the logs haven't been updated in a month. A. All reports and documentation that may contain sensitive data should be disposed of using secure disposal techniques. B. All items that are sold should have a bar code that can be scanned. C. All workstations should have authorization and identification controls, and employees should be trained to not share passwords. D. Sales transactions should be backed and logged immediately as transactions occur. A. Input and Origination Controls B. Output Controls	○	○	○	○	○	○
4.	Since Paul still has a lot to learn, he sometimes makes mistakes on his purchasing documentation and doesn't realize it until after the documents have been printed. When this happens, he hasn't really been trained on what to do, and he also doesn't want to advertise the mistakes. He's gotten into the habit of hiding any of the papers with errors, and just re-printing the corrected forms. A. All reports and documentation that may contain sensitive data should be disposed of using secure disposal techniques. B. All items that are sold should have a bar code that can be scanned. C. All workstations should have authorization and identification controls, and employees should be trained to not share passwords. D. Sales transactions should be backed and logged immediately as transactions occur. A. Input and Origination Controls B. Output Controls	○	○	○	○	○	○

4. Task-Based Simulation Solution

Work Tab	
	Help

Scenario	Control				Input or Output	
	(A)	**(B)**	**(C)**	**(D)**	**(A)**	**(B)**
1. Susan and Sarah are the only sales reps at ABC company, but when they get behind, they ask Paul, the purchasing intern to help take customer calls and create sales orders. He's not on their team, but they figure that it's good experience for Paul, and they need the help, anyway. A. All reports and documentation that may contain sensitive data should be disposed of using secure disposal techniques. B. All items that are sold should have a bar code that can be scanned. C. All workstations should have authorization and identification controls, and employees should be trained to not share passwords. D. Sales transactions should be backed and logged immediately as transactions occur. A. Input and Origination Controls B. Output Controls	○	○	●	○	○	●
2. Susan has a tendency to forget the inventory ID for some of the items that they don't sell too frequently. She tries to look them up every time, but sometimes she gets in a hurry and makes a guess. This results in some sales orders having the wrong inventory ID for what was actually sold. A. All reports and documentation that may contain sensitive data should be disposed of using secure disposal techniques. B. All items that are sold should have a bar code that can be scanned. C. All workstations should have authorization and identification controls, and employees should be trained to not share passwords. D. Sales transactions should be backed and logged immediately as transactions occur. A. Input and Origination Controls B. Output Controls	○	○	○	●	●	○

Scenario	Control				Input or Output	
	(A)	(B)	(C)	(D)	(A)	(B)
3. Greg, the database administrator, is supposed to be responsible for implementing a disaster recovery plan, but he's been extremely short-staffed lately. Even though the disaster recovery plan is documented and the sales system should be backed up weekly, the logs haven't been updated in a month. A. All reports and documentation that may contain sensitive data should be disposed of using secure disposal techniques. B. All items that are sold should have a bar code that can be scanned. C. All workstations should have authorization and identification controls, and employees should be trained to not share passwords. D. Sales transactions should be backed and logged immediately as transactions occur. A. Input and Origination Controls B. Output Controls	●	○	○	○	●	○
4. Since Paul still has a lot to learn, he sometimes makes mistakes on his purchasing documentation and doesn't realize it until after the documents have been printed. When this happens, he hasn't really been trained on what to do, and he also doesn't want to advertise the mistakes. He's gotten into the habit of hiding any of the papers with errors, and just re-printing the corrected forms. A. All reports and documentation that may contain sensitive data should be disposed of using secure disposal techniques. B. All items that are sold should have a bar code that can be scanned. C. All workstations should have authorization and identification controls, and employees should be trained to not share passwords. D. Sales transactions should be backed and logged immediately as transactions occur. A. Input and Origination Controls B. Output Controls	○	●	○	○	○	●

Answers and Explanations

1. **(C, B)** All workstations should have authorization and identification controls, and employees should be trained to not share passwords. Input and Origination Controls
2. **(D, A)** All items that are sold should have a bar code that can be scanned. Input and Origination Controls
3. **(A, A)** Sales transactions should be backed and logged immediately as transactions occur. Output Controls
4. **(B, B)** All reports and documentation that may contain sensitive data should be disposed of using secure disposal techniques. Output Controls

Operations Management

Cost Accounting

Overhead Variance Analysis

5. Task-Based Simulation

tbs.aq.ovhd.var.anls.001_0818

The responsibilities of the staff accountant at Roychester, Inc., a calendar-year corporation, include the quarterly completion of the quarterly budget versus actual variance analysis. Roychester's controller asks you to perform two tasks to assist in the variance analysis for the quarter ended September 30, Year 7.

Please note the following with respect to the variance analysis:

1. Roychester uses the accrual basis of accounting.
2. The Year 7 budget was finalized in October, Year 6. It did not include the expenses associated with the employee retreat announced in June, Year 7.
3. All recurring and adjusting journal entries have been posted to the general ledger unless otherwise noted.
4. All variance in excess of $1,500 or 5% of budgeted are investigated further at each quarter-end.

Task One:

Use the information provided in the exhibits to complete the quarterly budget versus actual variance analysis in the table below:

• In Column A, click in the associated cell and select the account that requires further analysis.
• In Column B, click in the associated cell and select the reason why the account selected in Column A requires further analysis.
• Not all rows may be needed to complete the table.
• A response in the option list for Column A may be used once or not at all.
• A response in the selection list for Column B may be used once, more than once, or not at all.

For CPAexcel Grading purposes:

1. In Column A, input Accounts requiring further analysis in alphabetical order.
2. If any rows remain unneeded after putting Accounts requiring further analysis in alphabetical order, click in each cell of the row and select "none" from the option list.

Income Statement - excerpt

Roychester, Inc. Income Statement Comparison - Selected Accounts (excerpt) For the quarter ended September 30, year 7		
G/L Account Name	**Actual**	**Budget**
Hourly - Wages	$326,450	$327,748
Fringe benefits	$232,564	$230,450
Office supplies	$3,575	$4,250
Professional fees	$25,000	$24,500
Miscellaneous	$3,850	$2,500
Totals	$591,439	$589,448

Fixed Asset Policy

Roychester, Inc.

Fixed Asset Policy: Depreciation (Excerpt)

Depreciation of fixed assets is computed on a straight-line basis over the estimated useful life of the asset as follows:

Asset class	Useful life
Buildings	40 years
Building improvements	20 years
Land improvements	15 years
Leasehold improvements	15 years
Computer equipment	3 years
Equipment	5 years
Furniture and fixtures	5 years
Large machinery	7 years
Office furniture	5 years
Software	3 years

The estimated useful life of a depreciable asset is the period over which services are expected to be rendered by the asset. Depreciation is calculated and recorded on a monthly basis for financial reporting purposes. Depreciation of assets commences when the asset is placed in service, with no depreciation in the month of disposal.

All asset classes have no salvage value.

Board Meeting Minutes

Roychester, Inc.
Board Meeting Minutes: July 15, year 7
9:00 AM, (via web conference)
(EXCERPT)

Members present:	F. Dobson (Chair)
	D. Almonsen
	R. Bhatacharia
	G. Kikugawa
	J. Osprey
Not present:	None
Agenda item:	**Sale of Building 1A**

The chair of the board of directors announced that the sale of Building 1A, which had been authorized in the January, year 7, board meeting (book value of $2,500,000), as well as the associated land (book value of $500,000), has successfully taken place. Settlement for the sale of the building and land was completed on July 6, year 7.

Agenda item: Acquisition of large finishing machine

The chair of the board of directors has introduced the following action item with respect to the need for a new large finishing machine:

- The current large finishing machine is fully depreciated and is in need of additional maintenance and repairs to keep it running efficiently.
- The proposal is to retire this asset, purchase a replacement, and place it in service by July 30, year 7.
- This purchase had not been anticipated when the year 7 budget was finalized.

Motion: Purchase replacement for fully depreciated large finishing machine.

APPROVED by quorum

Invoice - Machinery

Dayson Mfg. Equipment
8657 Maplewood Avenue
Elmer, NY 12354

Invoice 623
July 20, year 7

Sold to:
Roychester, Inc.
2480 Parkview Road
Raton, NY 12038

Model X-765 Finishing machine	$226,852
Sales tax at 8%	18,148
Total billed	$245,000
Deposit received upon ordering	(25,000)
Balance due upon delivery on July 25, year 7	$220,000

Thank you for your business!

Note from Controller: This asset was placed in service on August 1, year 7.

Email from President

From: president@roychester.com
To: Staff
Date: August 20, year 7 10:42AM
Subject: Appreciation for dedication and hard work

Team Roychester,

I want to thank all of you for your continued hard work and perseverance. We have had some challenges in trying to grow our business, and I sense that many of you could use a well-deserved break.

As a result, we will be offering a company-wide two-day retreat at Triple R Ranch next month. We hope this will rejuvenate and motivate you. All travel expenses will be covered by the company.

Further details will be available next week.

In the meantime, I thank you all for you continued dedication and hard work!

Regards,

J. Osprey
President, Roychester, Inc.
P. +1.222.322.1001
president@roychester.com

Property Insurance Invoice

Moredon Insurance Company
4700 Center Avenue
Suite 250
Raton, NY 12038

Invoice 1089
July 2, year 7

Insured:
Roychester, Inc.
2480 Parkview Road
Raton, NY 12038

Policy symbol	Policy number	Post date	Description	Account activity	Minimum amount due
PL	1258LR3	06/15/year 7	Property and liability (premium) effective 07/01/year 7 – 12/31/year 7	$5,500.00	$3,450.00
DUE DATE: 7/15/year 7			Service Charge		$3.00
			TOTAL DUE (minimum amount due)		$3,453.00
			TOTAL DUE (if paid in full)		$5,500.00

If minimum amount is paid, balance of $2,050 will be due on 8/30/year 7

Thank you for your business!

Budget Versus Actual Variance Analysis for the quarter ended September 30, year 7

Accounts requiring further analysis	Reasons for further analysis
1 A. Fringe benefits B. Hourly—Wages C. Miscellaneous D. Office supplies E. Professional fees F. None	A. The dollar value of the variance is greater $1,500, and the percentage value of the variance is greater than 5% B. The dollar value of the variance is greater than $1,500. C. The percentage of the value of the variance is greater than 5% D. None
2 A. Fringe benefits B. Hourly—Wages C. Miscellaneous D. Office supplies E. Professional fees F. None	A. The dollar value of the variance is greater $1,500, and the percentage value of the variance is greater than 5% B. The dollar value of the variance is greater than $1,500. C. The percentage of the value of the variance is greater than 5% D. None
3 A. Fringe benefits B. Hourly—Wages C. Miscellaneous D. Office supplies E. Professional fees F. None	A. The dollar value of the variance is greater $1,500, and the percentage value of the variance is greater than 5% B. The dollar value of the variance is greater than $1,500. C. The percentage of the value of the variance is greater than 5% D. None
4 A. Fringe benefits B. Hourly—Wages C. Miscellaneous D. Office supplies E. Professional fees F. None	A. The dollar value of the variance is greater $1,500, and the percentage value of the variance is greater than 5% B. The dollar value of the variance is greater than $1,500. C. The percentage of the value of the variance is greater than 5% D. None

Budget Versus Actual Variance Analysis for the quarter ended September 30, year 7

	Accounts requiring further analysis						Reasons for further analysis			
	(A)	(B)	(C)	(D)	(E)	(F)	(A)	(B)	(C)	(D)
1.	○	○	○	○	○	○	○	○	○	○
2.	○	○	○	○	○	○	○	○	○	○
3.	○	○	○	○	○	○	○	○	○	○
4.	○	○	○	○	○	○	○	○	○	○

Task Two:

The controller identified three additional accounts that require further analysis. Use the information provided in the exhibits to select an explanation for each variance identified by the controller in the table below.

In Column E, click in the cell and select the appropriate explanation for the variance identified by the controller in Columns A through D.

Expense account requiring further analysis according to the comptroller	Actual result	Budgeted amount	Variance	Explanation for variance			
				(A)	(B)	(C)	(D)
1. Depreciation	$86,457	$95,250	($9,793)	○	○	○	○
A. Decrease due to a decrease in expense from the addition of the finishing machine and a decrease in expense from the sale of Building 1A.							
B. Decrease due to a decrease in expense from the addition of the finishing machine and disposal of the old finishing machine and a decrease in expense from the sale of Building 1A.							
C. Decrease due to net effect of decrease in expense from the sale of Building 1A offset by an increase in expense from the addition of the finishing machine.							
D. Decrease due to net effect of decrease in expense from the sale of the land associated with Building 1A offset by an increase in expense from the addition of the finishing machine.							
2. Travel	$23,450	$9,000	$14,450	○	○	○	○
A. Increase due to expenses for board members traveling to board of directors meetings held during the quarter ended September 30, year 7.							
B. Increase to expenses for employee transportation to the company retreat and the increase in expense for board members travel board meetings held during the quarter ended September 30, year 7.							
C. Increase due to net effect of increase in expense for employee transportation to the company retreat offset by a decrease in expense for board member travel to board meetings.							
D. Increase due to net effect of increase in expense from board member travel to board of directors' meetings offset by decrease in expense for employee transportation to company retreat.							

Expense account requiring further analysis according to the comptroller	Actual result	Budgeted amount	Variance	Explanation for variance			
				(A)	(B)	(C)	(D)
3. Property and liability insurance A. Insurance premium of $5,500 correctly recorded in prepaid insurance. B. Insurance premium of $5,500 incorrectly recorded in prepaid insurance instead of $2,750 being recorded in insurance expense and $2,750 being recorded in prepaid insurance. C. Insurance premium of $5,500 incorrectly recorded in prepaid insurance instead of being recorded in insurance expense. D. Insurance premium of $5,500 incorrectly recorded in prepaid insurance instead of half of the minimum of the minimum amount due being recorded in insurance expense and the balance being recorded in prepaid expense.	$0	$2,750	$2,750	○	○	○	○

5. Task-Based Simulation Solution

Work Tab	
	Help

Budget Versus Actual Variance Analysis for the quarter ended September 30, year 7

Accounts requiring further analysis	Reasons for further analysis
1 A. Fringe benefits B. Hourly—Wages C. Miscellaneous D. Office supplies E. Professional fees F. None	A. The dollar value of the variance is greater $1,500, and the percentage value of the variance is greater than 5% B. The dollar value of the variance is greater than $1,500. C. The percentage of the value of the variance is greater than 5% D. None
2 A. Fringe benefits B. Hourly—Wages C. Miscellaneous D. Office supplies E. Professional fees F. None	A. The dollar value of the variance is greater $1,500, and the percentage value of the variance is greater than 5% B. The dollar value of the variance is greater than $1,500. C. The percentage of the value of the variance is greater than 5% D. None
3 A. Fringe benefits B. Hourly—Wages C. Miscellaneous D. Office supplies E. Professional fees F. None	A. The dollar value of the variance is greater $1,500, and the percentage value of the variance is greater than 5% B. The dollar value of the variance is greater than $1,500. C. The percentage of the value of the variance is greater than 5% D. None
4 A. Fringe benefits B. Hourly—Wages C. Miscellaneous D. Office supplies E. Professional fees F. None	A. The dollar value of the variance is greater $1,500, and the percentage value of the variance is greater than 5% B. The dollar value of the variance is greater than $1,500. C. The percentage of the value of the variance is greater than 5% D. None

Budget Versus Actual Variance Analysis for the quarter ended September 30, year 7

	Accounts requiring further analysis							Reasons for further analysis					
	(A)	(B)	(C)	(D)	(E)	(F)		(A)	(B)	(C)	(D)	(E)	(F)
1.	●	○	○	○	○	○		○	●	○	○	○	○
2.	○	○	○	●	○	○		○	○	●	○	○	○
3.	○	○	●	○	○	○		○	○	●	○	○	○
4.	○	○	○	○	○	●		○	○	○	●	○	○

Fringe Benefits requires further analysis because the dollar value of the variance is greater than $1,500. The Actual is $232,564 while the Budget is $230,450.

Office Supplies requires further analysis because the percentage value of the variance is greater than 5% of budget. The Actual is $3,575 while the Budget is $4,250, and the difference is actually over 15% of budget ($3,575 – $4,250) / $4,250.

The **Miscellaneous** account requires further analysis because the percentage value of the variance is greater than 5% of budget. The Actual is $3,850 while the Budget is $2,500, and the difference is actually over 50% of budget ($3,850 – $2,500) / $2,500.

Expense account requiring further analysis according to the comptroller	Actual result	Budgeted amount	Variance	Explanation for variance			
				(A)	(B)	(C)	(D)
1. Depreciation A. Decrease due to a decrease in expense from the addition of the finishing machine and a decrease in expense from the sale of Building 1A. B. Decrease due to a decrease in expense from the addition of the finishing machine and disposal of the old finishing machine and a decrease in expense from the sale of Building 1A. C. Decrease due to net effect of decrease in expense from the sale of Building 1A offset by an increase in expense from the addition of the finishing machine. D. Decrease due to net effect of decrease in expense from the sale of the land associated with Building 1A offset by an increase in expense from the addition of the finishing machine.	$86,457	$95,250	($9,793)	○	○	●	○
2. Travel A. Increase due to expenses for board members traveling to board of directors meetings held during the quarter ended September 30, year 7. B. Increase to expenses for employee transportation to the company retreat and the increase in expense for board members travel board meetings held during the quarter ended September 30, year 7. C. Increase due to net effect of increase in expense for employee transportation to the company retreat offset by a decrease in expense for board member travel to board meetings. D. Increase due to net effect of increase in expense from board member travel to board of directors' meetings offset by decrease in expense for employee transportation to company retreat.	$23,450	$9,000	$14,450	○	○	●	○

Expense account requiring further analysis according to the comptroller	Actual result	Budgeted amount	Variance	Explanation for variance			
				(A)	(B)	(C)	(D)
3. Property and liability insurance A. Insurance premium of $5,500 correctly recorded in prepaid insurance. B. Insurance premium of $5,500 incorrectly recorded in prepaid insurance instead of $2,750 being recorded in insurance expense and $2,750 being recorded in prepaid insurance. C. Insurance premium of $5,500 incorrectly recorded in prepaid insurance instead of being recorded in insurance expense. D. Insurance premium of $5,500 incorrectly recorded in prepaid insurance instead of half of the minimum of the minimum amount due being recorded in insurance expense and the balance being recorded in prepaid expense.	$0	$2,750	$2,750	○	●	○	○

For depreciation, the actual result was $86,457, the budgeted amount was $96,250, and the variance was ($9,793). The explanation for the decrease is due to the net effect of the decrease in expense from the sale of Building 1A offset by an increase in expense from the addition of the finishing machine. See the Fixed Asset Policy, Board Meeting Minutes, and Machinery Invoice Exhibits.

For travel, the actual result was $23,450, the budgeted amount was $9,000, and the variance was $14,450. The explanation for the variance is that the increase due to the net effect of the increase in expense for employee transportation to the company retreat is offset by a decrease in expense for board member travel to board meetings. See the Email from President Exhibit.

For property and liability insurance, the actual result was $0, the budgeted amount was $2,750, and the variance was ($2,750). The reason for the variance is that the insurance premium of $5,500 was incorrectly recorded in prepaid insurance instead of $2,750 being recorded in insurance expense and $2,750 being recorded in prepaid insurance. See the Property Insurance Exhibit.